THE CRISIS OF AMERICAN DEMOCRACY

THE CRISIS OF AMERICAN DEMOCRACY

THE PRESIDENTIAL ELECTIONS OF 2000 AND 2004

Four Lectures by David North

MEHRING BOOKS

© 2004 by Mehring Books
All rights reserved

UNITED STATES
PO Box 48377
Oak Park MI, 48237
Tel: 248 967 2924
Email: sales@mehring.com

AUSTRALIA
PO Box 367 Bankstown
Sydney, 1885
Tel: (02) 9790 3221
Fax: (02) 9790 3501
Email: mehring@ozemail.com.au

BRITAIN
PO Box 1306
Sheffield, S9 3UW
Tel: 114 244 0055
Email: sales@mehringbooks.co.uk

Web: www.mehring.com

ISBN 1-875639-36-5

Published by Mehring Books
Cover & text design by Pauline Haas
Cover flag image © David Carrick
Printed in Australia by BPA Digital Pty Ltd

1 2 3 4 5 6 7 8 9 10

Contents

Introduction

The election of George W. Bush to a second term as president of the United States came as a shock to millions of people around the globe and within the United States itself. It portends escalating US militarism abroad and an intensified attack on the democratic rights and social conditions of the American people.

The result poses profound political, and even moral, questions. The Bush administration dragged the American people into war based upon lies. It has presided over a massive transfer of wealth from the country's working masses to the financial elite, while carrying out the most far-reaching attacks on civil liberties in American history.

How was such an administration able to win a majority of the vote? And, why was the Democratic Party incapable of mounting an effective opposition to a government that came to power through the theft of an election, and has been mired in criminality and corruption ever since?

Most of what passes for political analysis of the 2004 American election, both in the United States and internationally, barely begins to pose such questions, much less answer them. Indeed, it rarely rises above the results of the latest opinion polls.

The lectures contained in this volume comprise a contemporaneous analysis of the political developments that produced both the Bush administration and its reelection—a first, best estimate of a rapidly changing political situation.

The value of the analysis is precisely what separates it from conventional studies of American politics. The central theme is that underlying the recent political upheavals lies an unprecedented growth of social inequality. The deepening class divisions find their reflection, however, in the electoral arena only in a distorted form, given the political monopoly exercised by two capitalist parties and the absence of any political party of the working class.

David North, chairman of the *World Socialist Web Site*'s international editorial board and national secretary of the Socialist Equality Party (SEP), develops this theme in four comprehensive lectures.

The first was delivered in December 2000, near the climax of the political crisis arising out of the disputed presidential election. The US Supreme Court was in the process of preparing its infamous decision installing a Republican administration that had been rejected by the majority of the American electorate.

North warns, "What the decision of this court will reveal is how far the American ruling class is prepared to go in breaking with the traditional bourgeois-democratic and constitutional norms."

Political developments since then have powerfully confirmed his prognosis. The launching of a war of aggression in defiance of mass opposition both in the US and across the globe has been combined with the arrogation of unprecedented police state powers by the White House. The Bush administration has asserted the right to jail anyone without charges or trial, on the sole determination of the president that the individual is an "enemy combatant." It has issued legal findings legitimizing torture, which found concrete expression in the grotesque photographs emerging from Iraq's Abu Ghraib prison.

North argues that the source of this ominous trend in American political life is an unprecedented polarization between wealth and poverty. Such deep social inequality is incompatible with democratic political forms.

The 2004 election—the subject of three of the lectures published in this volume—was held in the midst of a crisis provoked by mounting popular resistance to the US military occupation of Iraq.

As North explains, the war was the result, not merely of a conspiracy by a handful of extreme right-wing ideologues in the White House and the Pentagon. It represented a colossal failure of American democracy. The illegal invasion of a country that posed no threat to the United States was supported by both Democrats and Republicans, justified and even celebrated by the mass media and encouraged by powerful financial interests. It represented, in the final analysis, the attempt by US imperialism to offset the protracted decline in its relative strength on the world market through the use of military force. It was directed at establishing US control over those strategic oil reserves upon which its real and potential rivals in Europe and Asia depend.

In the course of the 2004 election, the Democratic Party emerged as a direct obstacle to the expression of mass antiwar sentiment. Even after Kerry belatedly began to criticize the Bush administration's handling of the war, the Democratic candidate repeatedly insisted that he would not seek the withdrawal of US troops from Iraq, but would, rather, escalate the military campaign in an attempt to crush the resistance. In the midst of the campaign, Kerry delivered his infamous statement that, even if he had known there existed no weapons of mass destruction in Iraq, or ties between Al Qaeda and Baghdad—the two false pretexts for the war—he still would have cast his vote to authorize the invasion.

The inability of the Democrats to mount a consistent opposition to the Bush administration on any social or political question is rooted in its class position. While passing itself off as a party of the people, it is controlled by, and defends, the interests of the financial elite.

North subjects the evolution of this party, from the Civil War period, when it sought to forge a perverse union between the slave owners in the South and the nascent working class in the North, through to the New Deal and the subsequent collapse and putrefaction of liberal reformism in the wake of the Vietnam War, to a careful historical analysis.

He argues that the 2000 and 2004 elections have demonstrated, above all, the terrible price that the American workers' movement has paid for its historic subordination to the Democratic Party.

"For American workers," North insists, "political wisdom begins with the understanding that their class interests cannot be achieved through the medium of a party that is controlled by, and subservient to, corporate interests, and that their most pressing task is to organize themselves as a politically independent force, in a party of their own, armed with a platform and program that clearly articulates their needs and aspirations."

The analysis presented in this volume was developed, not from the standpoint of academic contemplation, but as part of the Socialist Equality Party's active intervention in the 2004 elections. The SEP fielded candidates for president and vice-president—Bill Van Auken and Jim Lawrence—as well as congressional and local candidates.

The focus of its campaign was not so much the winning of votes, as the fight to politically educate the working class and develop its class consciousness. It began from the necessity of a political break with the Democratic Party and the building of a new mass independent party of the working class, based upon a program for the socialist reconstruction of society.

The Socialist Equality Party's internationalist perspective was expressed concretely in the decision to take its campaign to working people, students and intellectuals in Europe and Asia in the months leading up to the November 2 vote. One of the lectures published here was delivered to audiences in Australia and New Zealand. Other meetings were organized in Germany, Britain and Sri Lanka, to explain that none of the vital issues facing ordinary people in the US or any other country—war, employment, living standards, democratic rights—could be successfully confronted outside of a struggle to unite the working class across national boundaries against global capitalism.

In addition to the four lectures on the 2000 and 2004 elections, this book includes as appendices a political obituary of former US President Ronald Reagan, and an article marking the 40th anniversary of the assassination of John F. Kennedy.

The death of Reagan in June 2004 provoked an extraordinary reaction from America's political establishment. It mourned the passing of the former Hollywood actor as if he were the country's founding father. As North explains, the effusive tributes to Reagan represented a celebration by the ruling elite of its vast enrichment over the past quarter century and an appreciation of the reactionary social and political processes that the Reagan administration introduced, which facilitated the unprecedented concentration of wealth in the US.

The anniversary of Kennedy's assassination was marked by "sentimental hagiography extolling the legend of 'Camelot'" on the one hand, and "exercises in vituperation and character assassination from right-wing commentators" on the other. The article republished as Appendix 2 provides, instead, an historical overview of Kennedy's administration, linking his demise to internecine conflicts that have continued to rage at the heart of America's political system.

While the 2004 elections are over, they have not provided anything approaching political closure. The Bush administration's second term will unquestionably be a period of progressively deepening social, economic and political crises. The perspective provided in this volume will prove invaluable in orienting the inevitable political struggles to come.

BILL VAN AUKEN
New York
10 December 2004

LECTURE 1
Lessons from history: the 2000 elections and the new "irrepressible conflict"

3 December 2000

The political crisis in the United States, which erupted one month ago on Election Day, is made all the more dramatic by virtue of the fact that it was so completely unexpected.

Throughout the world, no country is seen as a greater exemplar of the power and stability of capitalism. The United States is still, in the minds of millions of people, the land of democracy, freedom and unlimited opportunity. And even among those who consider themselves critics of American imperialism: how many truly believe that a crisis could arise that would seriously call into question the stability of the entire system? How many of you would have been prepared to consider it possible, only a few months ago, that the United States would be hurled into a political crisis involving the entire governmental structure by the end of the year?

And yet here we are, one month after an election unlike any that has taken place in the United States in the twentieth century, and it is no longer unthinkable that the political system could undergo a dramatic and entirely unexpected transformation.

The beginning of a revolutionary crisis in the very bastion of world capitalism—and that is the essential significance of the present developments—has introduced into the world situation a factor of extraordinary and almost incalculable magnitude. Overnight, political strategists and economic theorists are suddenly confronted with a fact they would have considered unimaginable only four weeks ago: the political destabilization and possible collapse of the governmental structures of the United States.

Perhaps one of the most distinguishing features of a genuine crisis is that its arrival is generally unexpected and it assumes a form that could hardly have been predicted. This does not mean that it was altogether unforeseen. There was at least one organ of political analysis that had been insisting that the political structure in the United States was approaching a state of profound dysfunction—and that was the *World Socialist Web Site* (WSWS).[1]

As far back as December 1998, as the Clinton impeachment struggle approached its climax, the WSWS warned that the savage struggle between the Congress and the White House was a portent of approaching civil war.[2] But at that time the WSWS was a voice in the wilderness. We even received complaining letters from a number of our supporters protesting what they considered to be a tendency towards hyperbole or exaggeration.

HOW THE ELECTION CRISIS DEVELOPED

On November 7, 2000 approximately 100 million Americans—about half the potential electorate—went to the polls at the conclusion of what was, even by American standards, a more or less uneventful campaign. It had been anticipated during the final weeks that the outcome would be close, but no one was prepared for what actually took place.

Most commentators predicted that Bush would win. As the polls closed, however, it became clear that Gore and the Democrats were doing far better than expected in virtually all the major industrial states. The "battleground states" were going largely to the Democrats. Pennsylvania and Michigan, projected to be close, went to the Democrats by substantial margins.

But the biggest surprise of all came when the networks announced at 7:50 p.m. US Eastern Standard Time that Al Gore had carried the state of Florida. It appeared that the vice president was going to win the presidency.

Then a very strange series of events began. American politics has certain traditions. One is that on election night the presidential candidates are not heard from, except to either declare victory or concede defeat. And yet, after the networks had announced—based on exit polls that tend to be accurate—that the state of Florida was being given to Gore, an impromptu press conference was called in the mansion of Texas Governor George W. Bush. The Republican contender calmly and confidently declared that, notwithstanding predictions by the networks, ultimately he was going to win the state of Florida.

Bush's comments produced a strange impression. As I said, the press conference was a break with election night protocol. Moreover, not only was Bush making a premature and impromptu appearance to contest the networks' appraisal of the Florida exit polls, it was also reported that his senior campaign operatives were subjecting the networks to intense pressure, demanding that they change their call and take Florida out of the Gore column.

Why this was important would be revealed later. The political advantage that Bush would have in the days that followed was based almost entirely on the fact that the networks ultimately called the state of Florida for Bush, creating a public conception that he had won the election, regardless of the contest that was to follow.

At any rate, an announcement was made shortly after Bush's press conference that Florida was being taken out of Gore's column. Several hours later it was announced that Florida was being placed in Bush's column, and at about 2:00 or 2:30 a.m., Gore, having received the networks' revised projections, decided to concede the election.

Gore called Bush on the telephone, wished him well and said he would make his way to a public auditorium to deliver a concession speech. This was followed by even more extraordinary events. As Gore was making his way to the auditorium, the differences in the vote margins between Bush and Gore in Florida, which had been narrowing, began to drop rapidly. Desperate aides to the vice president contacted his motorcade via cell phone to inform him of this fact and to urge him to withdraw his concession. Apparently arguments ensued between the motorcade and the campaign headquarters. Gore was finally prevailed upon and he instructed his driver to turn around and return to the hotel room. He then called Bush and informed him that he was withdrawing his concession. Such things had never happened before. By the dawn of November 8, the only thing that was clear was that no one really knew who had won the election.

That evening marked the beginning of a chain of events without precedent in the history of the United States. While Bush clung to a lead of several hundred votes— out of a total of 6 million cast in the state of Florida—Gore enjoyed a majority in the overall popular vote—out of the 100 million cast in the US.

Reports began to emerge about irregularities in the Florida election. Somehow, it turned out, thousands of Jews in Palm Beach had voted for the notorious anti-Semite Pat Buchanan. One political wag said that this was probably because they had been thrilled by Buchanan's recent book praising Hitler. Information surfaced about African-American voters being harassed by state police on their way to polling places. At the same time, on thousands of ballots in predominantly Democratic precincts, there was apparently no vote registered for the office of president.

This set the stage for an ongoing and lengthy conflict over the counting of the Florida ballots. Much of this struggle has unfolded within courtrooms, culminating in the hearing before the US Supreme Court on Friday, December 1.

The conflict has also involved the use of mobs—hired by the Republican Party—to intimidate election officials, along with open appeals by the Republicans for the support of the military. As a result, one military official reportedly had to inform his officers that they were bound by the military code to remain aloof from politics.

A full and accurate count of all the ballots cast in Florida would have given the state, and therefore the national election, to Vice President Gore. The efforts of the Republican Party—supported by most of the media—have been centered on preventing such a count from taking place.[3]

All eyes are now focused on the US Supreme Court, which is expected to rule on Bush's appeal of a ruling by the Florida Supreme Court. That court rejected the initial certification of Bush's dubious victory by the Florida secretary of state, Katherine Harris, a Republican official and campaign co-chairman for Bush in Florida.

Even as it became clear that there were still thousands of votes to be counted and many issues unsettled, Harris insisted on certifying Bush's election victory. This was taken to the Florida Supreme Court, which, at the last minute, enjoined Harris against ratifying Bush's victory.

The legal issue was as follows: there are two statutes on the books in Florida; one states that the vote must be ratified by a certain day; another stipulates that there is a right of recount. Neither statute is written all that well, as often happens in legislative procedures, and one of the tasks of the court is to determine how it can reconcile conflicting legislative instructions.

The secretary of state is mandated by law to utilize discretion in observing the deadline—to consider all factors; not to blindly adhere to an arbitrary date set in the statute. The Florida Supreme Court overruled the secretary of state, declaring that the technical issue of a deadline was overridden by the fundamental questions of democratic rights raised by the election.

The Florida Supreme Court invoked the Florida Constitution's Declaration of Rights, which proclaims that the people have rights that cannot be infringed by the state. The justices asserted that "The right of suffrage is the pre-eminent right contained in the Declaration of Rights, for without this basic freedom all others would be diminished." The refusal of Harris to delay certification to permit a proper count of disputed ballots represented, according to the court, an arbitrary misuse of her discretion as a state official and, therefore, a violation of the Florida Constitution.

This ruling is currently being reviewed by the US Supreme Court. While a decision in favor of Gore, upholding the Florida Supreme Court, will not necessarily result in his election, a ruling against him would almost certainly bring the process to a conclusion and guarantee the ascension of Bush.

What the decision of this court will reveal is how far the American ruling class is prepared to go in breaking with traditional bourgeois-democratic and constitutional norms. Is it prepared to sanction ballot fraud and the suppression of votes? Is it prepared to install in the White House a candidate who has attained that office through blatantly illegal and anti-democratic methods?[4]

A substantial section of the American ruling elite, and perhaps even a majority on the Supreme Court, is prepared to do just that. This is because, among this social layer, there has been a dramatic erosion of support for traditional forms of bourgeois democracy.

One columnist summed up their cynicism toward democracy: "Yes," he wrote, "Gore probably got more votes, but who cares? Gore was mugged in Florida, but the local cops don't care."

WHAT IS THE NATURE OF THE CRISIS?

Notwithstanding the unprecedented character of the events of the last three weeks, political leaders and the media continue to insist—in direct contradiction to their actions and words—that the United States is not in the midst of a major constitutional crisis. The situation in America, the public is led to believe, is perhaps disturbing, but not too serious. The sowing of political complacency serves the interests of the ruling elite, which seeks to implement its political agenda, as much as possible, behind the backs of the people.

This complacency is echoed not only in what remains of

the politically flaccid liberal press, but also among the varied representatives of middle class radicalism. Ralph Nader, for example, has had virtually nothing to say about the post-election crisis, commenting in the most offhand manner that the dispute between Bush and Gore should be decided by the flip of a coin. Alexander Cockburn, the well-known left cynic, has announced himself pleased with the election result. Nothing more serious, he says, than several years of political gridlock in Washington. "First a word about gridlock," he wrote last week. "We like it." [5]

Then there is the position of the Spartacist newspaper, summed up in the following line: "The Gore-Bush feud at this point is more like a tempest in a tea pot than a political crisis of the bourgeoisie."

The wisdom of a political tendency in the United States called the Workers World Party is: "There is no social or economic crisis underlying the present election debacle."

If this is the case, recent events in America are completely inexplicable.

For the first time in the twentieth century it is impossible to determine the winner of a US presidential election. The vote reveals a completely polarized electorate. The virtual tie between Gore and Bush is mirrored in the composition of the Senate and the House of Representatives; and the election map resembles the division between the North and the South during the Civil War.

It has proved impossible to achieve a genuinely democratic adjudication of the post-election conflicts within the framework of the existing constitutional structures. And yet—we are assured by these people, who are the firmest believers in the stability of American capitalism—that none of this is related to a social or economic crisis! Such an assessment is the product of a combination of historical ignorance and political blindness.

LESSONS FROM HISTORY

From a formal standpoint, the only election bearing any resemblance to the present situation is that of 1876, when a conflict arose between the popular vote and the Electoral College result. The Democratic candidate Samuel Tilden won more popular votes. He probably had won more states and electoral votes as well, but, in a protracted political battle, the Republicans claimed the White House in exchange for making drastic political concessions to the old slavocracy in the South. This was the means by which Reconstruction was brought to an end.

But this analogy is inadequate to explain the significance of the present crisis. Let me repeat the argument of the liberals and middle class left, who assure us that nothing of any great significance has happened. They say it cannot be all that important because there is no fundamental social and economic crisis in America. People are in bad temper, they are fighting to get into office, everyone wants to win, but it is not all that important.

The representatives of liberalism and left radicalism would, I suspect, dismiss as absurd the claim that there exists within the United States the type of social and economic contradictions that could produce major political struggles, let alone a civil war. Prior to the 1860s, there was the "irrepressible conflict" between slavery and free labor. What possible social conflict could be said to exist today within the United States, comparable to the events of that time?

I will try to provide an answer to that question. But first, I would like to review, if only briefly, the way in which the political conflicts of the 1850s led ultimately to civil war.

During the past decade there has been a revival of interest in the American Civil War. Movies have been made and books written, some of them excellent, on this extraordinary chapter in American and world history.

The American Civil War was among the most important events of the nineteenth century. It had a profound impact on the development of the working class. It was in every respect one of the most heroic chapters in human history.

What a study of that period reveals is how the intensification of social contradictions—generated by the irrepressible conflict between the peculiar and archaic form of capitalism, based on slave labor, that prevailed in the American South, and the modern and dynamic form of capitalism based on wage labor in the Northern states—led to a complete breakdown of the political system.

For the first 70 years of the American Republic, this antagonism between two systems of labor, one slave and one free, constituted the ominous fault line beneath the entire political, social, economic and legal structure of the United States. Numerous attempts were made to find some means of containing the resulting political conflicts within the constitutional structure set up by the Founding Fathers. There was a profound desire to preserve the union. And yet events—social, economic and political—continuously conspired to intensify the underlying social contradiction, rendering impossible any political settlement.

For example, the balance between the slave and the free states was disrupted by the consequences flowing from the Louisiana Purchase of 1803, which added vast new tracts of land to the new republic. The early leaders of the United States had tried to deal with this through the Missouri Compromise of 1820, which set the Mason-Dixon Line as the boundary separating slave and free states. The compromise held for nearly 30 years. But the further expansion of the United States, especially as a result of the Mexican War of 1846–1848, instigated by the South, threatened to destabilize the balance of power between the free and slave states.

David Wilmot, a Congressman from Pennsylvania, introduced into the Congress in 1846 a proviso which demanded that no territory acquired by the US as a result of the Mexican War could be open to slavery. The South was vehemently opposed. One of the supporters of the Wilmot Proviso, a little-known congressman by the name of Abraham Lincoln, cast five votes in support of it in the course of his relatively brief congressional career. But Congress, which was dominated by the slave states, never accepted the proviso.

A battle erupted over whether California would be admitted into the Union as a slave or free state. Ultimately a compromise was hammered out and California became a free state. However, major political concessions were made to the slave owners, one of them being the Fugitive Slave Act, which demanded that all slaves escaping to the North be returned to their masters. Historian James McPherson gives a stirring account of the anger produced in the North by the sight of federal marshals entering cities like Boston, which had strong Abolitionist sentiment, grabbing ex-slaves and returning them to their former owners in the South.

There was a sense in the 1850s that the entire political structure was becoming destabilized by these conflicts. For those who opposed slavery and the growing power of the South, it was a very grim period. After one term in Congress, Abraham Lincoln left politics to devote himself exclusively to his career as a lawyer, becoming quite successful.

The event that was to lead to the radicalization of American political life was the Kansas-Nebraska Act of 1854. It opened up the possibility for the expansion of slavery into new territories north of the Mason-Dixon Line, profoundly altering the character of the American Republic. This not only undermined the position of free labor from an economic standpoint, but also called into question America's commitment to the democratic ideals that had been advanced in the Revolution of 1776. The Kansas-Nebraska Act declared that the nature of new territories admitted into the Union would be determined by a popular vote of the settlers. That is, Kansas settlers would vote on whether the constitution of the new state would be free or slave, and so determine how that state was admitted into the Union.

Stephen Douglas, a Democratic Party leader, also from Illinois, was the father of the concept of popular sovereignty. Douglas tried to reassure the North that even with this Act, given the nature of the climate and the geography of the North, there was little chance that the slave system, based on cotton, could expand northwards. And yet there was a sense that the Act had opened up the floodgates for an expansion of slavery beyond the Mason-Dixon Line. Indeed, the behavior of the Southern sympathizers who flooded into Kansas began to confirm the worst fears of their opponents.

The state became inundated with people known as Border Ruffians. They attacked free settlers and used terror to intimidate the anti-slave population. The political climate in the North became increasingly strained. All attempts to constrain political discourse within the norms of parliamentary politeness began to break down. In May 1856, an incident occurred that terrified the North. A respected Abolitionist, Senator Charles Sumner, who was seated in the Senate, was approached by a Southern congressman who proceeded to beat him with a cane to a bloody pulp, nearly killing him. The South hailed the act. The congressman responsible for the outrage was sent complimentary canes from his supporters in the South. The North viewed it as yet another manifestation of the barbarism of the slave states.

In 1857 the US Supreme Court handed down a deeply significant ruling. Dred Scott, a slave, had been taken north by his master and had lived in Illinois and Wisconsin, both free states. He traveled back with his owner to Missouri, which was a slave state. At that point he sued, insisting that because he had been taken into a non-slave state he could no longer be considered a slave. His suit began in the 1840s, but it was not until 1857, after more than 10 years of winding through the courts, that it finally came before the Supreme Court.[6]

An essential premise of the Missouri Compromise of 1820 had been that Congress had the right to restrict the expansion of slavery. The Supreme Court's decision in the Dred Scott case, therefore, was to have a fundamental effect on American political life. It more or less rendered civil war inevitable.

The court had a number of options. But what it finally ruled was that Dred Scott was a slave, not a citizen, and therefore had no standing to bring a suit against his owner. That was bad enough, but it did not stop there. The court went on to say that the fact that Dred Scott had been in a Northern state had no effect on his status as a slave—once a slave, always a slave.

The Supreme Court could have stopped there, too, but it

chose not to. It proceeded to declare, and this was what revolu-
tionized the United States, that an individual who was a slave
was a piece of property, which could be taken by its owner to
any part of the United States and remain a piece of property.

What did this mean? Aside from the horrifying moral implications—that slaves were not really human, but property—the
Supreme Court effectively nullified the Missouri Compromise.
It threw out what had been an operative constitutional premise:
that Congress had a right to restrict the expansion of slavery.
The court's decision meant that there existed no constitutional
restrictions on the expansion of slavery anywhere in the United
States. On this basis the Supreme Court satisfied the aspirations
and aims of the most aggressive and reactionary sections of the
Southern slavocracy to expand into new territory.

The decision came as a thunderbolt to Northern public
opinion. The Supreme Court was discredited for decades to
come, a not unimportant factor in Lincoln's decision to routinely ignore Supreme Court rulings during the subsequent civil
war. *Dred Scott* changed the entire face of American politics.
Lincoln, who by this time had been brought back into political
life by the Kansas-Nebraska Act, became one of the trenchant
critics of Douglas's theory of popular sovereignty. His following
grew as did the new Republican Party, itself a product of the
reaction against the Kansas-Nebraska Act and the *Dred Scott*
decision.

Examining this event, one sees a characteristic of ruling
classes when they sense the tide of history moving against
them. From the standpoint of the South, the growing industrial
and economic power of the North seemed a real threat. History
was moving against the slave owners, and the more they sensed
this, the more determined they were not only to protect slavery

in those areas where it existed, but to have slavery proclaimed a positive moral good, and to remove all restrictions on its expansion. In direct response to the growing social and economic weakness of the South, the political aggressiveness of its ruling class increased.

Another major event took place in the aftermath of the *Dred Scott* decision. An unrepresentative section of slave settlers, who were in a minority in Kansas, gerrymandered an essentially slave constitution known as the Lecompton Constitution and attempted to force it on the population of Kansas, most of whom were free settlers. A bitter controversy ensued. The slave settlers knew very well that the Lecompton Constitution would never be passed by a majority of Kansas voters. So they conspired to find a way to prevent it being sent for ratification by the people.

Various tricks and manoeuvres were used to find some means of ramming this thing down the throats of the free settlers. To make matters even worse, James Buchanan, the Democratic president from Pennsylvania, gave his political support to these reactionary efforts. It was only because of opposition in the House of Representatives that the Lecompton Constitution ultimately failed. Several years later, Kansas was admitted into the Union as a free state.

By 1860 it had become clear to the North that the South would not accept any restrictions on slavery: the South controlled the Congress and the Judiciary and it would not accept the loss of the presidency. The differences could not be peacefully resolved within the existing constitutional framework.

The election of 1860 revealed a completely polarized United States. Lincoln, the Republican candidate, did not receive a single vote for his candidacy in the 10 Southern states.

His victory in November 1860 was based on overwhelming support in the free states. It was immediately answered by a declaration of secession, first by South Carolina and then by a whole host of other Southern states. As Lincoln took office, much of the South was already in rebellion. By 1861, to borrow a phrase from James McPherson, Americans were shooting as they had voted in the election of 1860.

What could no longer be adjudicated was settled on the battlefield. At a cost of some 600,000 lives, the slave system was destroyed and the United States was reconstituted on the basis of bourgeois democracy—the abolition of slavery and the extension of citizenship to the entire population.

THE UNITED STATES IN 2000

Can any analogy be drawn between the crisis of pre-Civil War America and the situation today? Is there any social antagonism comparable to the one which underlay the "irrepressible conflict" that led to the Civil War?

Frankly, it is testimony to the extraordinary decline in the level of political thought, including among those who call themselves Marxists, that no-one detects the existence of such a social contradiction. But the fact remains that the United States today is the most socially polarized of the advanced capitalist countries. The lack of politically articulate forms of social struggle does not signify the absence of class struggle. Marx referred to "the class struggle, now open, now concealed". It has been concealed in the United States, but it rages beneath the surface.

Indeed, within the context of the extremes of social inequality, the absence of a politically conscious class struggle testifies, above all, to the intensity of the social oppression of the American working class. All the vast resources of corporate America are directed toward the political and ideological stultification of the masses of ordinary people. The present attack on the right to vote is only the inevitable political manifestation of the underlying tendency to systematically exclude the working class from any form of independent participation in political life.

It is important to examine the transcript of the Supreme Court discussion that occurred on December 1, and particularly the positions of Antonin Scalia, a disreputable and thuggish personality who argues with all the integrity of a mob lawyer. When questioning Laurence Tribe, counsel representing Al Gore, Scalia elaborated a thoroughly cynical justification for overruling the Florida Supreme Court.

Some of the arguments are complex, but I will try and explain the issue that has arisen. Let me give you an idea of the thinking of Scalia, which was shared by Chief Justice William Rehnquist, and certainly by Associate Justice Clarence Thomas—that is, by three out of the nine judges.

The issue is: does the Florida Supreme Court have the right to overrule an action by the secretary of state? The Republicans are arguing that the deadline is inviolable, that the Supreme Court in Florida has no right to change the rules. The argument of the Florida Supreme Court is that voting is a core democratic right that cannot be subordinated to administrative technicalities such as a filing deadline.

Scalia made the following argument. What is at issue in Florida is the selection of electors. That is, electors who will, in accordance with the procedures of the Electoral College, vote for one of the presidential candidates.

Allow me to explain the Electoral College. Americans do not vote directly for the president of the United States. The presidential election is actually the sum total of 51 local elections—50 state elections and one election in the District of Columbia. The candidate who wins the majority in each state generally is awarded the electoral votes of that state. And the electoral votes are proportional to, although not strictly based on, population. The larger states have more electoral votes than the smaller states. As it turns out, the smaller states are unduly represented because they automatically get an electoral vote for each of their two US senators. In Wyoming, 250,000 voters receive one electoral vote, while in New York there are approximately 500,000 voters per electoral vote.

Why has the anomaly of the Electoral College persisted? It was part of the federal arrangements, when the framework was being established to bring the various states of the United States together, to assure the smaller states that their voices would be heard. The Electoral College guarantees to each state a certain sovereign voice in the selection of the president. This was an important part of the Federal constitutional set-up—a complex division of power between the federal government and the states.

There was another argument behind the Electoral College, one that was not quite so noble. The Founding Fathers reasoned that there was always a possibility that the people might vote incorrectly; that they would choose a candidate of whom the ruling elites did not approve. There was an undercurrent in the writing of the Constitution that was profoundly anti-democratic, reflecting the outlook of representatives of a highly privileged social stratum. The Electoral College was an ultimate failsafe, a means for overruling the people should they vote the wrong way.

In actual fact, that never happened, and the Electoral College persisted as a quaint anachronism. It was never challenged, because the candidate who won a state election was entitled to send his slate of electors to the Electoral College. The popular vote corresponded with the Electoral College vote.

Let me return to the issues raised at the Supreme Court. Scalia begins musing that what is really involved in a presidential election is the selection of electors. He says that there is no right of suffrage in the selection of electors, that the people do not select electors. They are selected by the state legislature. Therefore, matters relating to the election of the president have nothing to do with the people, and it is totally inappropriate for the Supreme Court to begin invoking a declaration of rights to overrule a statute passed by the legislature. In the final analysis, he argues, there is no right of suffrage in the election of a US president.

Why does this raise the spectre of *Dred Scott*? As in 1857, Scalia is seizing the opportunity provided by Bush's appeal of the Florida Supreme Court's ruling to legitimize the most reactionary reading of the US Constitution. Just as Supreme Court Justice Roger Taney found in the *Dred Scott* case an opportunity to legitimize slavery throughout the United States, Scalia has used this case to deal a body blow against the most basic of democratic rights, the right to vote. He is introducing and legitimizing a profoundly anti-democratic interpretation of the American Constitution.

To be sure, the people do not vote directly for the president. But the Electoral College has persisted because the composition of its delegates corresponds to the popular vote within the states. The Electoral College would never have survived as a quaint anachronism of the American political system if its actions overturned the will of the people.

This is not just a speculative issue. Scalia, the political provocateur that he is, has actually been urging the Florida legislature to select pro-Bush electors, regardless of the outcome of the Florida vote. At the same time, he is elaborating an authoritarian, indeed, oligarchic conception of American democracy—or anti-democracy—that corresponds to what is acceptable to the most reactionary sections of the American ruling elite.

The question must be asked, what accounts for these extraordinary developments? Is Scalia just spinning theories? Or is there a social foundation for the contradictions that are now manifesting themselves in the political life of the United States?

To answer that question, I want to cite a passage from the Socialist Equality Party's election statement, published in the November 2000 issue of the *World Socialist Web Site Review.*

"At the top of American society is a possessing class richer, in terms both of wealth and income, than any in history. The richest one percent of American households has amassed more than $10 trillion in wealth—10 million million dollars— about 40 percent of the total national wealth. The combined net worth of these multimillionaires is greater than the total wealth of the bottom 95 percent of the population.

"Since the mid-1970s, the top one percent has doubled its share of the national wealth, from under 20 percent to 38.9 percent, the highest figure since 1929, the year of the stock market crash that ushered in the Great Depression. According to another study, the richest one percent of households owns half of all outstanding shares of stock, two thirds of all financial securities and over two thirds of business assets.

"The inequality in income is just as stark as the inequality in ownership. In 1999 the richest one percent of the population received as much after-tax income as the bottom 38 percent combined. That is, the 2.7 million Americans with the largest incomes received as much after-tax income as the 100 million Americans with the lowest incomes. The average after-tax annual income of the top one percent has soared by 370 percent since 1977, from $234,700 to $868,000."

The statement continues: "During the entire period of 1983 to 1995, these two elite layers, the rich and the super-rich, who make up the top 5 percent of the population, were the only households to experience an increase in financial net worth. This is a statistic worth reiterating: for 12 years straight, including part or all of the presidencies of Reagan, Bush and Clinton, the 'magic of the marketplace' resulted in a net loss for 95 percent of the American population, while only the top 5 percent gained ground.

"Throughout the 1990s a virtual mania for unearned income has gripped the ruling class, which has felt itself freed of any effective restraint on profit accumulation. The naked drive for personal wealth exceeds that in any previous 'Gilded Age'. CEO compensation rose a staggering 535 percent during the Clinton-Gore administration. The typical corporate boss makes 475 times the income of the average worker, and 728 times the income of a worker on the minimum wage. If wages had risen in the 1990s as fast as the salaries, bonuses and stock options enjoyed by CEOs, the average worker would have annual earnings of $114,000 a year, and the minimum wage would be $24 an hour."

This is a shocking picture of social inequality. To believe that democratic forms can be preserved in the midst of such extraordinary levels of social polarization is to simply ignore the lessons of history. The relationship between political forms and the class structure of society is of a complex dialectical character. But in the long run, there comes a point at which the social tensions produced by rampant social inequality cannot be contained within traditional democratic forms. American society has reached that point.

THE TWO-PARTY SYSTEM IN THE UNITED STATES

One of the peculiar features of American political life is the institutionalization of a two-party system that has persisted for nearly 135 years. The great weakness of the American workers' movement historically has been its inability to establish an independent political party. Political life has remained under the hegemony of the two bourgeois parties—the Democrats and Republicans—through which the political interests of the working class have been controlled and contained for more than a century.

Of course, these parties have themselves undergone significant changes during their long history. The Republican Party of today bears little resemblance to that which existed in the days of Dwight D. Eisenhower in the 1950s, let alone to that which existed under the leadership of Abraham Lincoln. Similarly, the Democratic Party has undertaken numerous makeovers—most significantly, when it forged an alliance, under the leadership of Franklin Delano Roosevelt, with the labor bureaucracy of the newly formed Congress of Industrial Organizations (CIO) and assumed a more explicit social-liberal character: at least in the North.

To trace the historical evolution of both parties is beyond the scope of this report. It must be said, and it is fairly obvious, that the center of gravity of American bourgeois politics has moved drastically to the right. Social liberalism, the dominant tendency for more than a half-century, has virtually ceased to exist. This must be explained, ultimately, from the standpoint of objective causes. Notwithstanding all the ballyhoo surrounding the strength of American capitalism, it has become ever less capable of accommodating the demand for social reform by the working class. The last significant piece of social legislation was put into effect about 30 years ago.

Yet, without offering anything in the way of substantial social reforms, the Democratic Party continues to present itself as the champion of the interests of working Americans. The Republican Party, on the other hand, has become, ever more openly, an organization of the extreme right. The unbridled rapacity of the most ruthless sections of the ruling elite, including those elements whose wealth derives from the market boom of the 1980s and 1990s, finds its most direct expression in the Republican Party.

If one were to attempt to sum up, in one sentence, the program of the Republican Party, it would be: "The Republicans seek the removal of all restraints—economic, political, social and moral—on the exploitation of labor, the realization of corporate profits and the accumulation of personal wealth."

This program was presented rather nakedly throughout the election campaign. Despite his various proclamations of "compassionate conservatism", Bush himself has presided over 135 executions in the state of Texas. He once said that making a decision on the death penalty was the most important question put before him. (It has since been substantiated that he devoted no more than 15 minutes to such matters). Underlying all the issues raised in the election was the distribution of social wealth.

In the United States there is no working class mass party. All political debate is funneled through two bourgeois and essentially reactionary parties. Yet these two parties cannot avoid becoming the focus of all social questions.

As socialists, we do not advocate a vote for any bourgeois party. We do not practise the politics of "lesser-evilism". Yet, we do not justify our opposition to the Democratic Party by claiming that it is merely the mirror image of the Republican Party. The strategic and programmatic conflicts within the ruling elite are fought out through these parties.

In the 2000 election campaign, the Democratic Party attempted—hypocritically, to be sure—to present itself as a party of the people. Gore would say, "I fight for the people, not the powerful." However inconsistently and disingenuously, Gore claimed to speak on behalf of the working people, and the issues that he raised—taxes, Social Security, medical care, education—were pitched to their interests. Implicit was the central question of the distribution and allocation of social wealth.

Bush's campaign centered on two demands: the lowering of personal income taxes and the abolition of the inheritance tax. Bush was rather shameless about this. In one debate he repeated again and again that his tax would overwhelmingly benefit the richest one percent of American society. "Why shouldn't it?" he argued, "they pay most of the taxes." His policy centered on an acceleration of the ongoing and massive transfer of wealth to the richest sections of society.

Significant sections of the working class did not necessarily perceive anything positive in the program of Gore, but they certainly recognized in Bush a threat to their social and democratic rights. There was in Florida and in the industrial states a massive turnout of black workers, far beyond what was expected.

The map of the 2000 election clearly demonstrates the social divisions within the United States. The Democratic vote was concentrated in the major industrial areas and the big cities. All those states that play a decisive role in the economic life of the US—California, New York, Pennsylvania, Michigan, Illinois—went for the Democrats. The Republican vote was concentrated in the South, the former bastion of the slavocracy, and in the upper-Midwest—generally speaking, the most backward parts of the United States.

The response of the Republican Party to the election, and to the conflict that followed, betrays an extraordinary aggressiveness and ruthlessness, which many commentators have found difficult to explain. Here again, it is valuable to draw attention to the outlook of this social layer.

Let me refer to an article written by Paul Craig Roberts, a right-wing commentator and member of the Reagan administration in 1980. He is apoplectic about the ongoing dispute over the election.

"Our country is being stolen. Geographically speaking, Gore carried only one-sixth of the country. Five-sixths of the United States rejected him and his corrupt party. Because of the population density of urban areas, maps showing election results by state greatly exaggerate Gore's geographical support.

"A map of the vote by county shows a tiny Gore presence. Gore's vote is confined to Hispanic counties in the Southwest, the California coastal counties, Portland Oregon counties, the counties bordering Puget Sound in Washington, Minnesota and urban areas of Great Lakes states, Jewish counties in Florida, heavily black counties in the Southeast and heavily urbanized areas of the Northeast (Philadelphia, New York City, Connecticut, Massachusetts, Rhode Island), Vermont and parts of Maine.

"Geographically, the map shows a country controlled by a few high-density urban counties where new immigrants and racial minorities constitute a high percentage of the population ... The Democratic Party is a party of well-to-do white liberals, university faculties and the media, single women and racial minorities. It is a revolutionary party, committed to over-throwing the 'hegemonic power' of traditional American morality, principles, institutions and people."

Roberts goes on to say: "Republicans will never get this hardened bloc vote. Blacks voted 90 to 93 percent for Gore, and Hispanics gave Gore between two-thirds and three-fourths of their vote. The longer the borders stay open, the sooner the country will be lost."[7]

The Republicans see a country, demographically and socially, that is moving, in objective terms, against them. They are becoming increasingly desperate and determined to use any means to retain the White House, and to utilize their control of the judiciary and Congress to beat back what they perceive as the growing threat of the masses.

WORLD DEVELOPMENTS AND THE AMERICAN CRISIS

In considering the significance of this situation, and in response to those who claim that there is no social or economic founda-tion for a major constitutional crisis, let me point out another similarity between the pre-Civil War decade and today.

Behind the political contradictions of that era were economic changes of the most colossal character. It was a period of extraordinary economic transformation—the emer-gence of industries, railroads, and telegraphs—the first signs of a modern industrial America.

Bruce Catton, a well-known historian, described the period thus: "The economic trend was unmistakable: every technological advance, the railroad, steamship, the telegraph, the new machines for farm and factory, pointed in a single direction, towards national unity and a complex industrial society and close integration with world economy. Rural self-sufficiency and isolation, except in detached pockets, had given way to commercial production for distant markets both national and international. A war in the Crimea or a panic on the Paris Bourse or a drop in interest rates by the Bank of England now touched off seismic shocks that rippled into the Monongahela textile mills and Pittsburgh iron foundries."[8]

Like the 1850s, the 1980s and 1990s have seen the profound transformation of the United States beneath the impact of revolutionary new technologies that have accelerated the process of globalization. The changes in social structure, the decline in the position of the traditional middle class, the vast proletarianization of society, are all bound up with these fundamental changes in the economic base of society. It is these processes that provide the most powerful impulse to the crisis that is now unfolding.

In the early 1990s, the International Committee of the Fourth International stressed that the breakdown of the USSR and the Stalinist regimes of Eastern Europe did not represent a failure of socialism, in as much as socialism never existed in those countries. Their autarchic national economies, the weakest national economies in the world, were collapsing under the pressure of global economic forces. Rather than representing a new stage in the flowering of world capitalism, the demise of these states was the product of global tendencies of economic development and crisis that would eventually shake the foundations of the advanced centers of world imperialism.

It took some time. There was the inevitable period of triumphalism: proclamations of the victory of world capitalism. And yet, while the wheels of history grind slowly, they grind exceedingly fine. The economic processes of globalization, which swept across the Soviet Union, blowing up the seemingly unchangeable institutions of Stalinist rule almost overnight, are now making their presence felt in the advanced sections of world capitalism, even the United States itself.

This is why, in the final analysis, the American crisis is a world crisis. In the political destabilization of American capitalism, accompanied by extreme economic dislocation, political events are intensifying the process of a serious economic downturn. Who can doubt that these events will have reverberations on an international scale?

Let me repeat a point I made at the beginning of my remarks. The great land mass against which all hopes of social revolution have been dashed, has been the United States.

The basic article of faith, for all those who have doubted or denied the viability of Marxism is that, ultimately, no matter what problem capitalism faces in any part of the world, Uncle Sam will always bail it out. The Federal Reserve has only to open up the spigots and the money will flow. Mexico can go bankrupt, but money will be quickly dispatched. Asia can go under, but something will be done to fix it up.

But what happens if the United States descends into a crisis that calls into question the stability of capitalist rule? No one has had to trouble themselves with such a question in the twentieth century. As we enter the twenty-first century, however, it has become the most critical issue.

Everyone, whether John Howard in Australia or Tony Blair in England, knows this is not a good thing for world capitalism. This is not a good time to ask Uncle Sam for money, let alone political advice. Who, in the aftermath of the Florida debacle, will want to hear from Jimmy Carter on how to run a democratic election?

These events not only have vast economic consequences. They will change the social psychology that plays an important role in the evolution of a revolutionary situation. In the end, the conscious factor assumes massive dimensions in the development of a revolution.

Leon Trotsky explained this so well. There is an objective component of a revolutionary crisis. When the forms of production come into conflict with existing social relations, a revolutionary epoch arises. But these objective contradictions must find their way into the consciousness of masses of people. People have to begin thinking about revolution. They have to want revolution and believe that revolution is a viable option. They have to feel not only the need, but also the possibility, of fundamental social change. In the final analysis, it is not the power of the capitalist state alone that blocks revolution. At a more profound and historically essential level, it is the lack of political confidence and consciousness, within the broad masses, of their ability to intervene and reconstruct society from top to bottom. But the present crisis will provide an impulse for significant and progressive shifts in social consciousness.

The events now taking place in America signify the end of that long period where the affairs of world capitalism could rest securely under the leadership of US imperialism. The United States will no longer be able to play that role. However protracted it proves to be, the 2000 presidential election marks a new stage in the crisis of American and, therefore, world capitalism.

LECTURE 2
The Iraq war, the Democratic Party and the campaign of Howard Dean

17 March 2004

The first anniversary of the United States' invasion and subsequent occupation of Iraq is only one week away. During the course of the past year the criminal character of the war has been exposed. The post-invasion search for Saddam Hussein's supposedly vast cache of toxic armaments produced absolutely nothing.

The propaganda campaign mounted by the United States over Iraq's "weapons of mass destruction" was nothing less than a state-sponsored exercise in mass deception. All the arguments made by the Bush administration to justify its decision to invade Iraq were based on lies. But the political establishment insists on characterizing the contradiction between reality and the government's sensationalist claims about WMD in Iraq as a mere "intelligence failure". This soporific euphemism facilitates the evasion of all the really serious political issues posed by the war.

What actually occurred last year? The president and vice president of the United States lied systematically and brazenly to the American people and to the world. These lies went

unchallenged within Congress, which passed a critical resolution, with the support of both John Edwards and John Kerry
that, for all intents and purposes, cleared the way for war.

The mass media, overwhelmingly pro-war, made no effort
whatever to subject the claims of the Bush administration to
any critical examination. Rather, it functioned as an amplifier
for the dissemination of government lies and misinformation.
The creation of a new title for reporters covering the war—
"embedded" journalists—captured, no doubt unintentionally,
the almost universal prostitution of the broadcast and print
media in the United States.

No, the war was not the product of a "failure of intelligence"—not even that of the intellectually handicapped
president. Rather, the war was the product, in a political sense,
of a historic failure, to the point of breakdown, of the institutions of American democracy.

Of course, the claim that the government was misled by
faulty intelligence—rather than that intelligence was rigged to
produce the results required by the Bush administration to justify a war it had already decided to launch—is completely
inconsistent with facts that were widely known by the time the
invasion of Iraq began. Although its intelligence-gathering net-
work is far less extensive than that of the corporate media, the
facts available to the Socialist Equality Party were sufficient for
us to draw the following conclusion on March 21, 2003:

"All the justifications given by the Bush administration and
its accomplices in London are based on half-truths, falsifica-
tions and outright lies. At this point, it should hardly be
necessary to reply yet again to the claims that the purpose of
this war is to destroy Iraq's so-called 'weapons of mass destruction'. After weeks of the most intrusive inspections to which any

country has ever been subjected, nothing of material significance was discovered. The latest reports of the leaders of the United Nations' inspection team, Hans Blix and Mohammed ElBaradei, specifically refute statements made by US Secretary of State Colin Powell during his notorious UN speech on February 5, 2003. ElBaradei exposed that allegations trumpeted by the United States about Iraqi efforts to import uranium from Niger were based on forged documents provided by British Prime Minister Tony Blair's intelligence services. Other major allegations, relating to the use of aluminum tubes for nuclear purposes and the existence of mobile laboratories producing chemical-biological weapons, were also shown to be baseless. As one lie is exposed, the Bush administration concocts another. So great is its contempt for public opinion that little concern is shown for the consistency of its own arguments."[1]

Despite massive popular opposition, expressed in huge demonstrations within the United States and throughout the world, the war began with the aerial bombardment of Iraq on March 19, 2003. As was explained in the statement from which I have already quoted:

"A small cabal of political conspirators—working with a hidden agenda and having come to power on the basis of fraud—has taken the American people into a war that they neither understand nor want. But there exists absolutely no political mechanism through which the opposition to the policies of the Bush administration—to the war, to the attacks on democratic rights, the destruction of social services, the relentless assault on the living standards of the working class—can find expression. The Democratic Party—the stinking corpse of bourgeois liberalism—is deeply discredited. Masses of working people find themselves utterly disenfranchised."

Though it encountered far greater opposition than it had expected, the overwhelming technical superiority of the American military resulted in the swift destruction of the Baathist regime and the occupation of Iraq. Intoxicated by its propaganda, the Bush administration and the media were utterly unprepared for the chaos that followed the entry of American forces into Baghdad and, somewhat later, by the outbreak of guerilla warfare against the occupation forces and their collaborators.

THE HOWARD DEAN CAMPAIGN

The media was no less surprised by the persistence and depth of hostility within the United States to the Bush administration. Projecting its own deeply-held class prejudices and illusions upon the general population, it assumed that the conquest of Iraq would more or less silence opposition to the war and guarantee the re-election of Bush. It failed, along with the bulk of the Democratic Party leadership, to anticipate the wave of popular opposition that found expression during the summer and autumn of 2003 in the presidential campaign of Howard Dean.

The Vermont governor was an unlikely leader of an insurgent movement. Dean did not create this movement; he sort of bumped into it as he groped about in the dark, like most conventional bourgeois politicians, looking for one or another issue that might distinguish him from his competitors. He sensed— and for this he must be given some credit—that there was an audience that would respond to attacks on the Bush administration, the war in Iraq, and the groveling cowardice that characterized the Democrats. Dean became a pole of attraction for the vast and untapped antiwar sentiment and hatred of

Bush that had gone largely ignored by the Democratic Party. Money poured into the coffers of the Dean campaign; polls indicated that the governor enjoyed massive leads in Iowa and New Hampshire and, by the end of 2003, the media began to consider seriously the possibility that Dean might actually win the presidential nomination.

This unexpected turn of events came as a wake-up call to the most politically astute sections of the ruling elite. It suddenly had become clear that popular opposition to the Bush administration was far deeper than they had previously believed. It was no longer inconceivable that Bush might actually fail to win re-election. Moreover, in addition to popular discontent, there had already begun to develop, within layers of the establishment itself, doubts and even anxieties about the policies, direction, consequences, and even competence, of the Bush administration. Not only issues related to the war in Iraq but, even more serious, the increasingly precarious state of the debt-ridden American economy began to set off alarms among those elements of the ruling class that had not completely lost their ability to think. By the beginning of the New Year, the possibility that Bush might lose the 2004 election came together with a sense, among significant layers of the ruling class that, perhaps, he *should* lose the election. The publication of former Treasury Secretary Paul O'Neill's memoirs, with its depiction of the president as an incompetent bully, was an expression of the changing mood within the bourgeois political establishment.

This shift in the political climate affected the coverage of the Democratic primary campaign. As long as 1) opposition within the ruling elite to the Bush administration remained politically negligible; and 2) Bush's re-election was taken for granted, the media covered the competition among Democrats with an air of bemused detachment. The prospect of Dean's nomination, followed inevitably by a devastating defeat, would not be entirely unwelcome. A Bush landslide might even serve to clean up the stench left by the 2000 election and, in addition, permit the government to claim that the invasion of Iraq had received popular ratification.

However, the new circumstances required a different and more intrusive approach to the Democratic primaries. Once again, the significance of the *bourgeois* two-party system—the historically tested instrument through which the capitalist class resolves its internal disputes, deflects mass opposition to the rule of the corporate oligarchy, and preserves its unchallenged monopoly of political power—was to be demonstrated.

Once the ruling elite concluded that the Democratic primaries might have something to do with selecting a replacement for the incumbent president, matters were quickly taken in hand. If Bush were to go, as a result of a combination of popular opposition and political dissatisfaction within the ruling elite, then the selection of the Democratic Party nominee would have to proceed with care.

The new orientation brought Dean's presidential aspirations to a rapid conclusion. Though he himself was a thoroughly conservative man, who represented no political threat to the system, his candidacy held open the possibility that the election might be seen throughout the world as a referendum on the war in Iraq, with far-reaching and dangerous implications for the interests of American imperialism. So the media decided, as the saying goes, to clean out Governor Dean's clock. And this conventional, though somewhat irascible, bourgeois from Vermont was entirely ill-equipped, intellectually and politically, for the assault that was launched early in the New Year.

Dean's efforts to reassure the media that he had no intention, despite his criticism of Bush's decision to launch the war,
of withdrawing US forces from Iraq anytime in the near future
was of no avail. The problem was not Dean's intentions, but
rather the danger that his candidacy might legitimize and
encourage, within the United States and internationally, opposition to the American occupation of Iraq.

In this context, permit me to cite a passage from a new document that was prepared by the bi-partisan Independent Task
Force on Post-Conflict Iraq, sponsored by the Council on
Foreign Relations. Entitled *Iraq: One Year After*, the document
expressed concern that popular support within the United
States for the long-term presence of troops in Iraq was fragile
and had to be buttressed.

"The Task Force believes that sustaining this public consensus is essential, especially as the political will of the United
States will continue to be tested in the months and years to
come in Iraq. These tests, which could include more high-
profile attacks on US troops, could come at a time of heightened
political debate in the United States, as we enter the final phase
of the 2004 election campaign.

"Iraq will unavoidably be a subject of debate during the US
presidential campaign. The debate will almost certainly encom-
pass the original decision to go to war as well as postwar political
transition and reconstruction efforts in Iraq. Nevertheless, Task
Force members, who represent a broad diversity of political perspectives, are united in their position that the United States has
a critical interest in a stable Iraq whose leadership represents
the will of the people. Civil conflict in Iraq, the alternative to
peaceful political competition [sic], would risk intervention by
and competition among Iraq's neighbors, long-term instability

in the production and supply of oil, and the emergence of a failed state that could offer a haven to terrorists. It would also represent a monumental policy failure for the United States, with an attendant loss of power and influence in the region."[2]

In other words, the election must not become a forum for a political debate that calls into question the legitimacy, and undermines public acceptance of, the United States' occupation. From this point of view, which sums up the bi-partisan consensus among the leaders of the bourgeois two-party system, Dean's nomination was unacceptable.

The attacks on Dean in the weeks leading up to the Iowa caucus, by both the media and his Democratic rivals, were effective, not so much because the voting public rejected Dean's policy. In fact, most polls showed that opposition to the war among Democratic voters in Iowa was overwhelming. Rather, the attacks exposed what Democratic voters perceived to be the weakness of Dean as a candidate in a national election. They resonated not only with those who already disliked him, but also with many who agreed with what they believed to be his antiwar positions—that is, with those who liked him, but who feared he would prove vulnerable to Republican attacks in the national election. In a peculiar way, the attacks on Dean successfully exploited the elemental desire of broad sections of the Democratic electorate to find a candidate who could defeat Bush.

With the unraveling of Dean's candidacy in the aftermath of the Iowa caucus and New Hampshire primary, the tone and character of the Democratic campaign rapidly changed. From that point on, the campaign was dominated by candidates who had voted for the Senate resolution that set the stage for the US invasion of Iraq. The eventual selection of Kerry as the nominee (though it might just as well have been John Edwards) guaranteed that the official election debate would proceed within parameters acceptable to the ruling elite.

THE PROBLEM OF THE DEMOCRATIC PARTY

One must say that this entire operation was carried out with extraordinary skill. The antiwar sentiment that had fueled Dean's campaign was rapidly deflated, and the nomination process ended up with the selection of a candidate whose differences with Bush on Iraq, as well as all other critical questions, were of an essentially tactical, rather than principled, character.

How could this happen? It is not enough to speak of the role of the media. Its manipulation of public opinion is successful to the extent that the political thinking of the working class remains within the confines of the bourgeois two-party system. The only means by which the broad mass of workers can express their latent discontent with bourgeois politics is by abstaining entirely from the electoral process—which is precisely what half to two-thirds of the voting population does in every election. This extraordinary level of political abstention can only be understood as a manifestation of the deep alienation of tens of millions of Americans, probably a majority, from the entire political set-up. They do not participate in the electoral process because they do not see in it a means of improving their own lives.

At the same time, alongside indifference, there are to be found illusions, of which the most debilitating and ultimately demoralizing is the belief that somehow the Democratic Party represents, in some vague sort of way, a genuine alternative to the Republican Party. This illusion is essential to the durability of the bourgeois two-party system in the United States.

Where there are illusions, there are usually illusion-makers—that is, individuals, organizations and political tendencies that devote themselves to shoring up confidence in the two-party system, especially the Democratic Party. By way of example, one of the more intriguing aspects of the Democratic primaries was the enormous publicity that was given to the candidacies of Congressman Dennis Kucinich and the most pious reverend Al Sharpton.

Week after week, in one debate after another, these two worthies were allowed a platform alongside the other candidates. The fact that their votes in the various primary states generally were below three percent did not result in a revocation of their invitations to the debates. They were afforded the opportunity to make their criticisms of the corporations and mouth all sorts of left phrases. But in return, they proclaimed their faith in the Democratic Party as the sole legitimate agency of political progress in the United States.

In the end, their participation served to nourish the illusion that the Democratic Party is a genuine "people's" party, fundamentally opposed to the Republican Party, susceptible to mass pressure, and capable of carrying out significant, if not radical, reforms of American society in the interests of working people.

Howard Dean did exactly the same upon announcing the conclusion of his campaign for the presidency. He urged his supporters to avoid any involvement in third-party politics, and to continue working for change in the Democratic Party.

Of greater political significance than the statements of Kucinich, Sharpton and Dean—who, after all, have lived their political lives within the Democratic Party and have no direct association with anti-capitalist politics—has been the stance of the *Nation*. This voice of American middle-class radicalism— whose record of political foulness stretches all the way back to the 1930s, when it supported Stalin's extermination of Marxist revolutionaries in the Soviet Union—is now supporting the candidacy of John Kerry.

The most detailed exposition of its position in support of the Democratic candidate came in an open letter to Ralph Nader, published in the *Nation* of February 16, in which it urged him not to declare himself a presidential candidate in 2004. "Ralph," it wrote, "this is the wrong year to run: 2004 is not 2000."

What is the difference?

"George W. Bush has led us into an illegal pre-emptive war, and his defeat is critical ... The overwhelming mass of voters with progressive values—who are essential to all efforts to build a force that can change the direction of the country—have only one focus this year: to beat Bush. Any candidacy seen as distracting from that goal will be excoriated by the entire spectrum of potentially progressive voters. If you run, you will separate yourself, probably irrevocably, from any ongoing relationship with this energized mass of activists."

Thus writeth the *Nation*!

The Socialist Equality Party and the *World Socialist Web Site* have fundamental and irreconcilable differences with the politics of Ralph Nader. But those differences do not include opposition to his decision to run for president. He has every right to do so, even if his campaign subtracts from the votes of the Democratic candidate and costs Senator Kerry the election.

The arguments made by the *Nation* are politically and

intellectually bankrupt. Its basic argument is that the difference between 2004 and 2000 is that the defeat of Bush's re-election must be the overriding political goal of all "progressives". But if that is true, does it not follow that everything should have been done in 2000 to prevent Bush from getting elected in the first place? This would mean, of course, that Nader's decision to contest the presidency four years ago, which the *Nation* supported, was a disastrous mistake.

The *Nation* makes no effort to resolve this glaring contradiction. Rather, it attempts, in a manner that is both absurd and contemptible, to glorify Senator Kerry. It writes of his "courage, devotion to justice and commitment to honesty, open government and principles-over-politics. There are few senators of whom that can be said."

That such nonsense can be written in 2004 testifies to the impoverished state of what is called radical politics in the United States. After all, Mr. Kerry is hardly an unusual political specimen. No special powers of political analysis must be brought to bear to understand that he is a determined and unwavering defender of the social interests of the ruling elite and the capitalist system as a whole.

Moreover, the specific features of Kerry's personality are of negligible political significance. In the elaboration of a principled position in this election campaign—that is, one that upholds the interests of the working class—it is necessary to proceed from an historical evaluation of the bourgeois two-party system and, in particular, the class character of the Democratic Party.

The problem of the Democratic Party has bedeviled the socialist movement in the United States since its earliest days. The most significant feature of the American labor movement—

noted by socialist theorists since the days of Marx and Engels— has been its failure to establish itself as a politically independent force.

The working class in the United States has, in the course of its history, engaged in struggles that have, not infrequently, assumed truly explosive dimensions. Its strikes were often accompanied by a level of violence unknown in European countries, except during periods of outright civil war. And yet, in contrast to its class brothers and sisters in Europe, the American working class never succeeded in freeing itself from the domination of the political parties of the bosses whom it was fighting bitterly in the factories and the streets.

Every generation of socialists in the United States has confronted this problem and sought to resolve it—first and foremost, through the development of a mass, politically conscious, anti-capitalist, socialist political party. There have been periods of intense class struggle, when it appeared that a breakthrough was both possible and in the offing—during the pre-World War I upsurge of the working class, during the Great Depression of the 1930s, in the immediate aftermath of World War II and, finally, in the late 1960s and early 1970s. In each instance, however, a combination of objective and subjective factors aborted these promising movements by the working class toward political independence.

An examination of this critical problem obliges us to return to the issue of the Democratic Party. This has been the principal instrument employed by the American bourgeoisie for more than a century to block the development of an independent working class party, preserve the hegemony of the bourgeois two-party system, and maintain the capitalist class' monopoly of political power.

This is not the place to attempt a substantial review of the history of the Democratic Party. The content of such an examination would consist, more or less, of the entire political history of the United States. After all, according to some accounts, the origins of the Democratic Party are to be found in political factions that arose during George Washington's administration in the 1790s.

However, there is one persistent feature of the Democratic Party that must be noted. From the time that it first emerged in its quasi-modern form, that is, in the 1830s, the Democratic Party sought to cast itself as the defender of the common workingman against business interests. This characteristic was celebrated by historian Arthur Schlesinger, Jr., in his book *The Age of Jackson*. Seeking to counter socialist influence in the working class, Schlesinger argued that Jackson's administration, in its use of state power to curb powerful financial interests, provided the model for liberal democratic rule that found its apotheosis in Franklin Roosevelt's New Deal.

What Schlesinger conveniently glossed over was that Jackson's hostility to Northern business interests stemmed not from genuinely progressive sentiments, but, rather, reflected the reactionary outlook of the Southern slave-owning class. The susceptibility of sections of urban workers to Jackson's cynical exploitation of their grievances for the purpose of luring them into an alliance with the slave-owners was an early symptom of what was to prove a fundamental weakness of the workers' movement in the United States: its attempt to find short-term solutions to profound social problems on the basis of corrupt political alliances with representatives of one or another section of the ruling class.

Schlesinger's *Age of Jackson* was published in 1944, near the end of Roosevelt's long tenure as US president. Though several generations separate us from the era of Roosevelt, and his memory has largely faded from the consciousness of broad masses of the American people, his four terms in office were critical in burnishing the popular credentials of the Democratic Party. Roosevelt's New Deal, as it entered into political folklore, retold again and again by the trade union bureaucracy, marked the phoenix-like rebirth of social justice in America. It was, supposedly, an era of unprecedented social progress, the result of Roosevelt's radical restructuring of American capitalism.

The reality was quite different. Roosevelt certainly displayed extraordinary political acumen in adapting his administration to the deep popular hostility to capitalism engendered by the Depression. But his policies were, for the most part, palliatives that hardly came to grips with the deeper causes—rooted in the contradictions of the world capitalist system—of the devastating economic crisis. The most important gains made by the working class were those it achieved in the course of direct struggles, usually in the face of opposition from the Roosevelt administration. The second economic collapse of 1937 exposed the failure of the New Deal, and unemployment remained at nearly 25 percent until the entry of the United States into World War II in December 1941.

THE LABOR PARTY DEMAND

By the mid-1930s, the eruption of mass working class struggles—such as the Toledo Auto-Lite strike, the Minneapolis general strike, the San Francisco general strike, and, somewhat later, the Flint sit-down strike—brought to the fore the issue of independent political action by the working class. The newly-formed Congress of Industrial Organizations (CIO) began to confront, more and more, the limitations of militant trade unionism. Strike action alone could not solve the issues of industrial democracy, social equality, and the dangers posed by fascism and imperialist militarism.

Especially as workers began to confront ever more bitter resistance from the employers—exemplified by the massacre of Chicago workers on strike against Republic Steel on Memorial Day 1937—trade union militancy appeared increasingly as a blind alley. Moreover, the escalating hostility of the Roosevelt administration to workers' struggles for unionization—Roosevelt had infuriated unionists by responding to the Memorial Day massacre with a denunciation of *both* strikers and employers ("A plague on both your houses," declared the president, quoting Shakespeare)—called into question the legitimacy and viability of the CIO's de facto alliance with it and with the Democratic Party. The CIO was little more than two years old, but it had already arrived at an impasse.

This was the situation that formed the background to a series of extraordinary discussions held in Coyóacan, Mexico, in May 1938, between leaders of the Socialist Workers Party—at that time, the Trotskyist movement in the US—and Leon Trotsky, the exiled leader of the 1917 October Revolution and founder of the Fourth International. The problems of the CIO, he argued, required a turn toward political struggle. He urged the Socialist Workers Party to initiate a campaign within the new trade union movement for the formation of a labor party.

"It is an objective fact," Trotsky argued, "that the new trade unions created by the workers came to an impasse—a blind alley—and the only way for the workers already organized in

trade unions is to join their forces in order to influence legislation, to influence the class struggle. The working class stands
before an alternative. Either the trade unions will be dissolved
or they will join for political action."[3]

As Trotsky emphasized in the course of these discussions,
he was not advocating the formation of a reformist party such
as the British Labour Party. Rather, the fight for a labor party was
indissolubly connected with the raising of transitional demands
that directed workers toward a struggle for power. The labor
party demand was aimed against the political subordination of
the working class to the Democrats by the trade union bureaucracy and the Stalinists of the Communist Party.

The introduction of the labor party demand into the program of the Socialist Workers Party marked a critical advance in
the development of a revolutionary strategy for the American
working class. It identified the central problem of the labor
movement in the United States—its subordination to the political parties of the bourgeoisie—and showed a way forward. The
fight for the formation of a labor party brought the Trotskyist
movement into ever more intense conflict with the trade union
bureaucracy of both the American Federation of Labor (AFL)
and CIO which, whatever their differences, were determined to
maintain the subordination of the working class to the
Democratic Party.

In the aftermath of the Second World War, workers' living
standards improved dramatically. While these gains were taken
by the labor bureaucracy as a vindication of its political alliance
with the Democratic Party, they were, more profoundly, the
result of the vast postwar expansion of the world economy.
Far more significant than what the American workers won
was what they lost—that is, the opportunity to fundamentally

transform the social and economic structure of American society in the interests of the working class.

From the beginning, in the period of Roosevelt, the alliance with the Democratic Party meant, above all, the repudiation by the trade unions of any radical-democratic, let alone revolutionary socialist, aspirations. All talk within the trade union movement of a radical redistribution of wealth within the United States, of the democratization of the work place, of the right of workers to inspect corporate finances, and of the establishment of state control over industry—which all had been popular demands in the 1930s—had to be stopped. This necessarily entailed the suppression of dissent within the trade unions, which was generally achieved through the use of goon squad violence and political purges.

The historian Alan Brinkley has summed up very well the political implications of the labor movement's subordination to Roosevelt and the Democratic Party:

"[In] its new partnership with democrats, liberals, and the state, trade unions were destined to be a subordinate force, incapable of shaping the liberal agenda in more than marginal ways." [4]

There were other consequences, for which the working class was to pay a devastating price. The United States had emerged from World War II as the principal imperialist power. Its far-flung interests made it uncompromisingly hostile to any restraint on the ability of American corporations to exploit the resources of the globe. In the name of defending liberal democracy, the American labor movement not only fell into line behind the Cold War launched by the United States in 1946, it provided the most fervent warriors in the global crusade against communism and every manifestation of anti-imperialist struggle. The activities of the international department of the AFL-CIO became largely embedded in the work of the CIA itself. Without the anti-communism legitimized by the AFL-CIO, McCarthyism would have never been able to get off the ground within the United States.

There is yet another significant aspect of the postwar alliance with the Democratic Party that was to have far-reaching consequences. As the power structure of the postwar Democratic Party in the 1940s and 50s was still based partially on the Jim Crow apartheid system that prevailed in the "Solid South", the labor bureaucracy politely refrained from any determined effort to unionize workers in that part of the country. Thus, the great civil rights movement of the 1950s and early 1960s developed independently of the labor movement.

The AFL-CIO's reactionary abstention from, and hostility to, the struggle against Jim Crow in the South, and the democratic and social aspirations of African-American workers in the North, ceded leadership of the civil rights movement to various sections of the black middle class. Rather than developing as part of a powerful class struggle for democratic rights and social equality, the civil rights movement ultimately degenerated into a striving for privileges among a small section of the black middle class within the framework of capitalism.

By the 1960s, both the Democratic Party and the AFL-CIO had both entered into crisis and decline. The eruption of the civil rights movement destroyed the equilibrium between the liberal wing of the Democratic Party in the North and its segregationist wing in the South. The gradual end of the postwar boom and the deterioration of the United States' unchallenged economic supremacy began to expose the limitations of the Keynesian policies upon which the reformist programs of the postwar period had been based. And finally, the catastrophe of the Vietnam War—which was itself the product of the Cold War strategy devised principally by the Democratic Party—left American liberalism divided, morally compromised and discredited.

The trade union bureaucracy, tied to the Democratic Party, had always assumed that the resources of American capitalism were inexhaustible, and that the never-ending expansion of the national economy would provide an enduring foundation for reformist policies.

But as that perspective was shattered by the economic crises of the 1970s—by the simultaneous eruption of recession and inflation, or "stagflation", as it was known at that time—the AFL-CIO had no alternative to the class war policies introduced by the Federal Reserve chairman, Paul Volcker, who had been appointed by the Democratic president, Jimmy Carter, in 1979. The AFL-CIO was unprepared for the political and social consequences of the collapse of American liberalism, the resurgence of the Republican Party, and the onslaught against the trade unions that was unleashed in 1981 with the firing of 11,000 members of PATCO, the air traffic controllers' union. It accepted the massive restructuring of American industry that was to cost the jobs of millions of industrial workers over the next two decades.

The labor bureaucracy sabotaged every attempt by workers to defend their jobs. The list of strikes betrayed by the AFL-CIO in the 1980s encompassed virtually every section of the organized working class. By 1990, it became increasingly clear that the AFL-CIO was, in fact, the apparatus of a section of the middle class that served as a secondary agency for the exploitation of the working class. It could no longer be described, in any realistic sense, as an organization of the working class.

Just 55 years had passed since the formation of the CIO. Only 35 years had passed since the consolidation of the AFL and CIO into a single trade union federation that was the largest and richest in the world. But within that very short period of time, its policy of class collaboration, its political alliance with the Democratic Party, its furious war against any semblance of socialist ideology in the working class, had resulted in the complete shipwreck of the American labor movement. It was once said that without Marxism there is no workers' movement. This was proven by the AFL-CIO.

THE POLITICAL BASIS OF THE SEP CAMPAIGN

Based on all the lessons of the history of the American working class, the Socialist Equality Party emphatically and unequivocally rejects the claim that the most burning task in 2004, to which all other concerns and considerations must be subordinated, is the defeat of President Bush.

No, the most pressing and urgent task is to fight for the political independence of the working class on the basis of a socialist and internationalist program. The problem of Bush must be solved by the working class itself. It must advance its own solution and not farm this out to various sections of the ruling elite.

In insisting upon this principle, we do not minimize the reactionary and criminal character of the Bush administration. Unlike the *Nation*, we understood very well the new quality represented by the assault on democratic procedures, first in the impeachment campaign and then in the aftermath of the 2000 election. But that does not change our principled outlook as to how such dangers are to be fought.

We recognize that the policies of the Bush administration arise from a crisis of the entire world capitalist system that will deepen, and become still more dangerous, regardless of who wins the next election. For the SEP, the election campaign is not simply about what to do in November. It is about the political preparation that is necessary for what will follow the election.

Those who tell the working class today that it should give its vote to the Democratic Party and John Kerry must accept responsibility for the consequences of that political advice. What will they say to workers if Kerry should happen to win the election? What political credibility will they have when that administration, acting in accordance with the pressure of the class interests it represents, undertakes further military action in the pursuit of the imperialist interests of the United States? Or when it attacks the working class?

What changes will follow from the election of Kerry? Will there be any basic shift in the strategic orientation of American imperialism? Will it alter the fact that the policies of the US are driven by certain global imperatives? Will it remove the objective geo-strategic imperative, which underlies the present policies of the Bush administration, to secure control of Middle Eastern and Central Asian oil and other critical and scarce natural resources? Will the election of Kerry produce a withdrawal of American troops from the Middle East or Central Asia?

As for American economic policy, how would it be altered, in any fundamental sense? The destruction of jobs and the decline in living standards will continue. Is it conceivable that a Kerry administration would dare to initiate an assault on the bastions of wealth that are so fundamental to the social structure of the United States and the social policy that prevails?

No serious change in social conditions within the United

States is possible without a direct assault on accumulated private wealth. That will not be undertaken by a Democratic administration, nor will the Democrats begin a struggle against the great corporations that rule this country. There will be no reduction in the unprecedented concentration of wealth, within the top one percent of society, that has occurred over the past 20 years.

As in every election year, the Democratic candidates posture as "friends" of the working people. But the demagogic character of these professions of concern is most clearly exposed when they are compared to promises made in decades past. Almost exactly 40 years ago, on May 12, 1964, at the University of Michigan, Lyndon Johnson unveiled his Great Society. He stated:

"The challenge of the next half century is whether we will have the wisdom to use [America's] wealth to enrich and elevate our national life, and to advance the quality of our American civilization ... For in your time we have the opportunity to move not only toward the rich society and the powerful society, but upward to the Great Society ...

"The Great Society rests on abundance and liberty for all. It demands an end to poverty and racial injustice, to which we are totally committed in our time. But that is just the beginning."

How has the promise to eliminate poverty been realized? When Johnson gave this speech, with perhaps a certain element of sincerity, the entire liberal agenda was about to disintegrate at the very apex of the postwar expansion of capitalism.

But Johnson, seeing nothing but rainbows as he approached the abyss, considered the elimination of poverty to be "just the beginning" of the Great Society. The "Great Society" he predicted never got started. The conditions that exist today make a mockery of his illusions in the future of a capitalist America.

Just a few days ago, the *Detroit Free Press* published statistics on the income of residents of Detroit's midtown area. According to the *Free Press*, 39.1 percent of the residents of midtown Detroit earn less than $10,000, and 21 percent earn between $10,000 and $19,999—that is, 60 percent of these residents are living at or below the official poverty line. Another 14 percent have an annual income of between $20,000 and $29,999. This means that nearly 75 percent of the population of midtown Detroit is earning less than $30,000 per year.

Another report, on poverty in New York City, was released by the Community Service Society last September. It cited data from the US Bureau of the Census indicating that 12.1 percent of Americans live in poverty—that is, more than 30 million people. In New York City, the poverty rate is over 20 percent. Still another report, by the same organization, summarized data on unemployment among black males in New York. It found that 48.2 percent of black men of working age were unemployed.

None of these deep problems can be addressed by capitalism. What is required is a revolutionary restructuring of the American and world economy.

Forty years ago, socialists might have criticized, with full justice, the Great Society program as mere palliatives. But there is no place for such palliatives in the agenda of modern day capitalism. In fact, there has not been a significant piece of reform legislation passed in the American Congress since the 1960s.

At the same time, there has been a massive growth in the apparatus of state repression. Some 43 years ago, in January 1961, President Eisenhower warned about the intrusion of the military industrial complex. But what he called the military industrial complex in 1961 would look like a toy army of tin soldiers from today's perspective.

The fight for democracy is impossible without the independent political mobilization of the working class. Even the achievement of such essential and necessary reforms—which are not even socialistic—as the abolition of the Electoral College and the establishment of a new voting system based on the principle of proportional representation—are unthinkable without a mass movement in opposition to the principal beneficiaries of the capitalistic two-party system, the Democrats and Republicans.

The fundamental task to which we address ourselves—the building of a genuine workers' movement—is possible only on the basis of a socialist program.

We say to those, like the liberals or the radicals of the *Nation*, who claim that they are doing something "real" in 2004, that they are, rather, wasting time, misleading the working class, and postponing the essential task.

Whatever the outcome of this election, the ability of the working class to defend its rights and defeat the preparations for further wars depends on the development of a new perspective and a much higher level of political class consciousness. This is what we will be fighting to achieve during the 2004 US presidential election campaign.

LECTURE 3
Militarism and social polarization in contemporary America
5 September 2004

For reasons that are not difficult to understand, the outcome of the 2004 presidential election is being awaited with intense interest all over the world—indeed, perhaps with greater concern outside the US than within it. There is a sense that the United States is a dangerous country, controlled by ruthless and reckless militarists who will stop at nothing to achieve their global aims. And this is not an opinion with which I would argue.

The gathering of the Republicans in New York City, commencing on August 30, to renominate George W. Bush as their presidential candidate bore a greater resemblance to a Nazi Party rally in Nuremberg than to the typical convention of a bourgeois-democratic political party in the United States. Outside the convention, on the streets of New York, nearly 2,000 people were swept up and arrested by police in massive dragnets organized to prevent or break up political protests.

Inside the convention, a reactionary mob cheered wildly as they listened to fascist-style speeches delivered by the likes of Vice President Dick Cheney—the once and future bagman for Halliburton, who now presides over a secret government about which the American media says nothing—and Senator Zell Miller from Georgia, a Democrat, who speaks for that section of the Democratic Party that is supporting, either openly or covertly, the reelection of George Bush.

It was in Miller's speech that the anti-democratic, authoritarian, militaristic and imperialistic outlook, which is rampant within the ruling elite, found its most precise expression. He said that, "It is the soldier, not the reporter, who has given us freedom of the press. It is the soldier, not the poet, who has given us the freedom of speech." As a matter of historical fact, this is absolutely wrong. The first great blow for freedom of the press was struck in colonial America by a journalist, Peter Zenger. And without the poetry of Tom Paine, not to mention that of Tom Jefferson, it would not have been possible to muster the citizen-patriots who were prepared to sacrifice their lives for the cause of independence and liberty. Of course, the media did not call attention to the absurdity of Miller's statement, which is further contradicted by the legal theory that forms the basis of the US Constitution and its evolution. Miller's remarks cannot be dismissed as merely the ravings of a right-wing political lunatic; for the past three years have seen a determined effort by the government to legitimize the use of military tribunals in which civilian defendants are stripped of all constitutional rights, including habeas corpus.

This brings me to another statement made by Miller in his address before the Republican Convention:

"No one should dare to even think about being the Commander in Chief of this country if he doesn't believe with all his heart that our soldiers are liberators abroad and defenders at home."

This declaration falsifies the content of the US Constitution and the intent of its framers. But Miller's statement is not in any way original or exceptional. The frequent assertions by politicians and media types that the president is the country's "commander in chief" is intended to disorient the people, undermine their natural democratic instincts, and legitimize the drift toward a military-police dictatorship.

According to Article II, Section 2, Clause 1 of the US Constitution, "The President shall be Commander in Chief of the Army and Navy of the United States, and of the Militia of the several states, when called into the actual service of the United States ..." There is nothing ambiguous about this clause: the president is the commander in chief not of the country as a whole, but of the military. He is the country's principal elected magistrate, not its fuehrer. The correct usage of the president's auxiliary title underscores the domination of the elected civilian representatives of the people over the military, rather than the military over the civilian branch of government. Miller's speech is merely one example of the degree to which basic concepts of democracy have become utterly alien to the American ruling class.

We are not dealing with merely a process of intellectual degeneration. The relentless accumulation of wealth in a very small stratum of the American people has the inevitable impact of narrowing the real social base upon which bourgeois rule rests. The ruling class is compelled to create another base, consisting of elements that stand outside of, and are, to a considerable extent, independent of, the broad mass of the people. This is the role of the volunteer army, which is supplemented by gangs of contract killers and torturers hired by the military to augment the forces of repression in Iraq and Afghanistan. The experience of urban warfare in Iraq, where American soldiers become accustomed to and, in some cases, even acquire a taste for, killing and repressing civilians on a mass scale, is creating a dangerous social type upon which the ruling elite will increasingly depend to maintain "law and order" in the United States.

Some of you may recall that I spoke in Sydney nearly four years ago, in the immediate aftermath of the balloting in the November 2000 election. It was December 3, 2000, and the results of the election were still unknown. I said at the time that the outcome of the election would reveal the extent to which there still existed a commitment to traditional forms of bourgeois democracy in the United States. Less than two weeks later, the Supreme Court intervened to stop the recount of disputed Florida ballots, and selected George W. Bush president of the United States. That event marked a turning point in American history. Its worldwide implications have since become clear.

The events of the last four years have changed profoundly global perceptions of the United States. Even for those who were not inclined to view American society through rose-tinted glasses, and knew better than to accept uncritically Washington's endless professions of its democratic and benevolent ideals, recent developments have come as a shock. The invasions of Afghanistan and Iraq have provided examples of the sort of unbridled imperialism that the world has not witnessed since World War II. The grotesque images of sadism displayed in the photographs taken in Abu Ghraib prison will define, for an entire generation, the brutal and predatory essence of the American occupation of Iraq.

In politics, as with life in general, people have a natural inclination to hope that simple and easy solutions can be found to difficult and serious problems. Herein lies the appeal of the notion that the election of John Kerry as president of the United

States will, if not fundamentally transform, then at least lead to an improvement in the overall international political climate. Those who would like to believe this proceed from the conception that present American policy is to be explained by the personal characteristics of the occupant of the White House. Ironically, this conception transforms Bush, an ignorant nonentity, into something akin to a world historical figure.

But the "Bad Bush Theory of History" can provide no guide to an understanding of, let alone a solution to, the great problems of our day. Even if Kerry were to win this election—despite the cowardly and bankrupt character of his campaign—it would not alter, in any significant manner, the destructive and barbaric trajectory of American imperialism. It would not bring the occupation of Iraq to an end. It would not lessen the likelihood of further, and even more destructive, wars in the near future.

Even if one were to grant that the conduct of American foreign policy is shaped, to some extent, by criminal aspects of the personalities of Bush and his coterie—and it certainly is—this subjective factor is of secondary importance. After all, the very fact that Bush's policies have enjoyed such broad support within the political and social establishment of the United States demonstrates that factors far more substantial than the personality disorders of the president are involved in the formulation of state policy.

The invasion and occupation of Iraq represents a colossal failure of American democracy. This war was launched, as everyone in the world now knows, on the basis of out-and-out lies: 1) that there existed weapons of mass destruction in Iraq; 2) that the regime of Saddam Hussein was allied to Al Qaeda and, by implication, somehow involved in the events of 9/11;

and 3) that the United States was seeking to bring democracy to Iraq.

Prior to the invasion of March 2003, none of these claims was subjected to serious examination by the political establishment or the mass media. The oversight was not an accident. To the extent that the bellicose policies of the Bush administration enjoyed broad support within the ruling elite and both of its major political parties, there was no interest in making a searching examination of the reasons advanced by the government for going to war. This political reality is underscored by the fact that the subsequent exposure of the lies has led to no significant erosion of political support for the continued occupation of Iraq within the ruling elite. The recent declaration of Senator Kerry that he would still have voted for the notorious Senate resolution of October 2002, authorizing the use of force against Iraq, even had he known then that there were no weapons of mass destruction in that country, is a crushing refutation of the argument that the policies of the Bush administration represent some sort of aberrant departure from a more restrained and moderate course of American foreign policy.

In justifying its own policies, the Bush administration endlessly invokes the specter of September 11, 2001. Indeed, in the modern mythology of American politics, that date occupies an exalted place. After 9/11, as the phrase goes, "everything changed". This is one of those universally accepted truisms that does not bear too careful scrutiny.

The events of 9/11 played no significant role whatever in determining the international strategy of the United States. Any moderately knowledgeable observer of American foreign policy could have anticipated, well before September 11, 2001— indeed, well before the installation of Bush as president in

January 2001—that the invasions of both Afghanistan and Iraq by the United States were inevitable.

The entire direction of American foreign policy since the conclusion of the first Gulf War was calculated to justify a resumption of war against Iraq. Similarly, the invasion of Afghanistan was anticipated by the growing preoccupation of American policy makers, throughout the 1990s, with the geo-strategic and economic significance of Central Asia. It was none other than Zbigniew Brzezinski, the former national security adviser of President Jimmy Carter, who, in his book entitled *The Grand Chessboard*, written in 1997, argued that America's global position in the twenty-first century depended on achieving a dominant role in Central Asia. Acknowledging the substantial social costs that protracted American military involvement in Central Asia would impose upon the American people, Brzezinski warned that domestic support for such actions would be difficult to achieve "except in conditions of a sudden threat or challenge to the public's sense of domestic well-being."[1]

September 11 did not lead to a reformulation of American foreign policy. Rather, it provided a *pretext* for the realization of geo-strategic ambitions formulated and pursued by US administrations dating all the way back to that of Jimmy Carter.

It is worth restating the essential geo-strategic aims that underlie the wars launched during the Bush administration and, lest this be forgotten, the war launched by President Bill Clinton against Serbia in 1999.

The principal objective of the three presidential administrations (Bush I, Clinton, and Bush II) which have held office since the dissolution of the USSR in 1991 has been to exploit the historic opportunity provided by the Soviet collapse to establish an unchallengeable hegemonic position for the United States in world affairs. As early as 1992, the US military issued a new strategic document, in which it proclaimed that the goal of American policy was to prevent any state from being able to challenge, economically or militarily, the dominant position of the United States.

Within the context of this global strategy, the domination of the Middle East and Central Asia—with their vast reserves of oil and natural gas—constitutes an absolute imperative. For the United States, unrestricted access to, and control of, these reserves—which represent a substantial portion of all known world-wide reserves—is critical not only to guarantee the satisfaction of its own domestic energy needs. In a world where the depletion of oil and natural gas reserves over the next quarter century is a critical issue, control over the distribution and allocation of these reserves would give the United States a stranglehold over the fate of all present and potential competitors.

With regard to this essential strategic aim—the establishment and consolidation of American hegemony in world affairs—there exists no significant or fundamental difference between George Bush and John Kerry. To the extent that differences do exist, they are principally of a tactical character—that is, over the degree to which the United States should be prepared to adapt its pursuit of hegemony to some sort of international imperialist multilateral framework.

But even those who are critical of Bush's conduct of foreign policy recognize that a change of administration will not fundamentally alter its unilateralist direction. As Professor G. John Ikenberry has written:

"With the end of the cold war and the absence of serious geopolitical challengers, the United States is now able to act alone without serious costs, according to the proponents of unilateralism. If they are right, the international order is in the early stages of a significant transformation, triggered by a continuous and determined effort by the United States to disentangle itself from the multilateral restraints of an earlier era. *It matters little who is president and what political party runs the government: the United States will exercise its power more directly, with less mediation or constraint by international rules, institutions, or alliances. The result will be a hegemonic, power-based international order. The rest of the world will complain but other nations will not be able or willing to impose sufficient costs on the United States to alter its growing unilateral orientation"* (emphasis added).[2]

This conclusion is undoubtedly correct, for, notwithstanding his tepid criticisms of the unilateralism of the Bush administration, Kerry continuously emphasizes that his administration would not hesitate to act unilaterally if that were deemed necessary in the "national interest".

Ikenberry bemoans the accelerating tendency toward unilateralism, but he fails to explain the reason for its development. He refers repeatedly to the immense military superiority of the United States over all other national states, stressing that this essential geo-political fact allows the US to ignore, if it chooses, international opposition to whatever policies it decides to pursue. But this explanation is inadequate. After all, in the immediate aftermath of World War II, when the military and economic superiority of the United States was at its zenith, the Truman administration was preoccupied with creating a complex of international multilateral structures.

When World War II came to a close, the dominant position of the United States in the structure of international capitalism was guaranteed far less by military power than by its massive and, at that point, unchallengeable economic superiority. The supreme symbol of American power was not the atomic bomb, but the dollar. The entire framework of international finance and trade rested on the dollar, which functioned as the world reserve currency, convertible into gold at the rate of $35 per ounce. The financial and industrial power of the United States provided the essential resources for an immense expansion of world economy.

The world situation today is vastly different. The global economic position of the United States has weakened dramatically during the past 60 years. Even by 1971, the relative weakening of the United States vis-à-vis its principal capitalist rivals in Europe and Japan brought about the collapse of the Bretton Woods system and its linchpin, dollar-gold convertibility. During the ensuing decades, the United States has been transformed from the world's creditor into its greatest debtor. Sixty years ago, American industrial and financial power fueled the rebuilding of a world capitalist order that had been shattered by depression and war. Today, the viability of the American financial system depends upon the willingness of foreign states and investors to finance the country's staggering current accounts deficit.

The United States is now borrowing approximately $540 billion per year to cover its rapidly expanding current accounts deficit. This amounted to 5.4 percent of gross domestic product (GDP) during the first quarter of 2004, which is far higher than the previous record of 3.5 percent of GDP in 1987, when the dollar lost more than one-third its value and the stock market crashed.

There is a general consensus among bourgeois economists that the current accounts deficit—whose largest component is the negative balance of trade—is leading to a serious crisis. Many expect that a substantial decline in the dollar, with potentially destabilizing consequences internationally, is both unavoidable and necessary.

According to Peter G. Peterson, chairman of the Council on Foreign Relations:

"The next dollar run, should it happen, would likely lead to serious reverberations in the 'real' economy, including a loss of consumer and investor confidence, a severe contraction, and ultimately a global recession ...

"Virtually none of the policy leaders, financial traders, and economists interviewed by this author [Peterson] believes the US current account deficit is sustainable at current levels for much longer than five more years. Many see a real risk of a crisis. Former Federal Reserve Chairman Paul Volcker says the odds of this happening are around 75 percent within the next five years; former Treasury Secretary Robert Rubin talks of 'a day of serious reckoning'. What might trigger such a crisis? Almost anything: an act of terrorism, a bad day on Wall Street, a disappointing employment report, or even a testy remark by a central banker."[3]

The noted economic analyst of the *Financial Times*, Martin Wolf, describes the situation in even blunter terms: "The US is now on the comfortable path to ruin. It is being driven along a road of ever-rising deficits and debt, both external and fiscal, that risk destroying the country's credit and the global role of its currency. It is also, not coincidentally, likely to generate an unmanageable increase in US protectionism. Worse, the longer the process continues, the bigger the ultimate shock to the dollar and levels of domestic real spending will have to be. Unless trends change, 10 years from now the US will have fiscal debt and fiscal liabilities that are both over 100 percent of GDP. It will have lost control over its economic fate."[4]

Recognition of its own deteriorating global economic position is a significant factor in the increasing reliance of the United States on military force. But, paradoxically, the vast cost of America's far-flung military operations is yet another major burden weighing down the national economy. The operation in Iraq is a case in point. It costs the United States one billion dollars every week to keep two divisions engaged in "stability operations". To keep them engaged for a whole year would cost the entire GDP of New Zealand.[5] And the costs of the Iraq war are additional to the already vast sums of money ear-marked for military spending. According to recent calculations by the Congressional Budget Office, the Bush administration has seriously underestimated the amount of money that will be required to fund military outlays over the next decade. An additional $1.1 trillion dollars in new spending will have to be allocated.[6]

Even more significant than the financial strains generated by the cost of American militarism is its destabilizing and potentially explosive impact on inter-imperialist and inter-state relations. The drive by the United States for hegemony does not take place in a geo-political vacuum. To the extent that the ambitions of the United States impinge on the vital interests of other states, confrontation and conflict is unavoidable.

The recriminations between the United States and Europe during the run-up to the invasion of Iraq reflected real conflicts over material interests. At some point these conflicts can lead to more than sharp diplomatic exchanges. In the end, "Old Europe" bit its lip and watched glumly as the United States invaded Iraq. But will it do the same as the US, in pursuit of new sources of oil, seeks to shove Europe aside in Africa? In July 2002, Assistant Secretary of State Walter Kansteiner declared during a visit to Nigeria that "African oil is of strategic national interest to us." The Bush administration has identified six African oil producers as being of critical importance to the energy policy of the United States: Nigeria, Angola, Gabon, the Republic of Congo, Chad and Equatorial Guinea (the latter being the target of a plot, masterminded by none other than Sir Mark Thatcher, the son of the illustrious former prime minister of Britain, that was exposed in March 2004). And there are now discussions within the Defense Department about establishing a new African Command to coordinate the actions of the US military on that continent.[7]

Aside from potential conflicts with old imperialist rivals, the American thrust into Central Asia during the past five years increases the potential for military conflict with all other states with major interests in the future of that region, including Iran, India, China and Russia.

Let us grant that certain aspects of American foreign policy may be affected by a change of personnel in the White House, State Department and Pentagon. A Kerry administration may, perhaps, devote greater effort to winning the endorsement of its imperialist allies for one or another military action. But such differences are in the style, not in the substance, of policy. The violent and aggressive character of American capitalism—like that of German capitalism in the 1930s and 1940s—is only the most extreme expression of the essentially predatory character of the imperialist system. Within the framework of a capitalistic world system, the fundamental contradiction between world economy and the nation-state system cannot be managed peacefully.

In May 1940, as Hitler's armies swept across France, Leon Trotsky rejected facile explanations for the eruption of the war: "The present war—the second imperialist war—is not an accident," he wrote. "It does not result from the will of this or that dictator. It was predicted long ago. It derived its origin from the contradictions of international capitalist interests. Contrary to the official fables designed to drug the people, the chief cause of war as of all other social evils—unemployment, the high cost of living, fascism, colonial oppression—is the private ownership of the means of production together with the bourgeois state which rests on this foundation ... So long ... as the main productive forces of society are held by trusts, i.e., isolated capitalist cliques, and so long as the national state remains a pliant tool in the hands of these cliques, the struggle for markets, for sources of raw materials, for the domination of the world, must inevitably assume a more and more destructive character." [8]

How appropriate, timely and prescient these words are today! The vast and powerful economic forces that shape and determine the policies of American imperialism will not be altered by a mere change of personnel in Washington. The debate between Bush and Kerry over how best to realize the global ambitions of the United States is one that is taking place within the ruling elite, that small fraction of American society in which the vast bulk of national wealth is concentrated. The concerns of millions of ordinary working class Americans—who are, for the most part, against war—find absolutely no genuine expression in the official campaigns of either of the two imperialist parties.

JOHN KERRY AND THE "LEFTS"

To imagine that the direction of American policy will be significantly changed by the replacement of Bush by Kerry is to indulge in the most pathetic illusions. But there seems to be no shortage of such illusions among those who consider themselves on the "left". For example, Mr. Tariq Ali—who back in the 1960s and 1970s was among the principal leaders of the International Marxist Group in Britain, and who still describes himself as a socialist—is calling for a vote for Kerry. Mr. Ali's record as a political analyst does not inspire confidence. In the late 1980s, when he was enthusiastically promoting Perestroika and Glasnost as a great advance for socialism in the Soviet Union, he dedicated a book that he had written on this subject to none other than Boris Yeltsin, "whose political courage has made him an important symbol throughout the country."[9] But let us not dwell on the past. Rather, let us turn to what Tariq Ali has to say now about the American elections.

Interviewed on August 5 by WBAI Radio in New York City, Tariq Ali asserted that the defeat of Bush would send a positive message overseas. "A defeat for a warmonger government would be seen as a step forward," he said. "I don't go beyond that, but there is no doubt in my mind that it would have an impact globally."

In what sense would the election of Kerry be a step forward, and what would be the global impact of this development? Would it be followed by a withdrawal of US troops from Iraq? Would it bring about the withdrawal of US troops from Afghanistan? The answer to these questions is, unequivocally, no. As for the global impact of Bush's defeat, it might actually facilitate efforts by the United States to win European support for the occupation of Iraq, and for other military actions that are in the planning stage. This, in fact, is one of the arguments that Kerry is making as he seeks to convince influential sections of the ruling elite to throw their support behind his candidacy.

Another argument for supporting Kerry appeared in the August 16 issue of the *Nation*. Explaining why she has finally joined the "Anyone But Bush" camp, Naomi Klein offered this novel argument: Bush is so hated by "progressives" that as long as he is president, it is impossible for them to think seriously about politics and the deeper causes of the war and the general crisis of society.

"This madness has to stop," she writes, "and the fastest way of doing that is to elect John Kerry, not because he will be different but because in most key areas—Iraq, the 'war on drugs', Israel/Palestine, free trade, corporate taxes—he will be just as bad. The main difference will be that as Kerry pursues these brutal policies, he will come off as intelligent, sane and blissfully dull. That's why I've joined the Anybody But Bush camp: only with a bore like Kerry at the helm will we be finally able to put an end to the presidential pathologizing and focus on the issues again."

Does such an argument even merit an answer? Discovering that all her friends have lost their heads, Ms. Klein has decided to join their company by removing her own.

There is a term which encompasses the sort of politics practiced by the Tariq Alis and Naomi Kleins of this world. It is *opportunism*, by which we mean the subordination of fundamental questions of political principal to pragmatic and purely tactical calculations. Indifferent toward theory (which they dismiss as merely "abstract") and history, opportunists habitually evade the difficult problems of political development. When challenged by Marxists, who criticize their refusal to work through the implications of their tactical prescriptions from the standpoint of the independent political organization of the working class and the development of socialist class consciousness, the opportunists justify their pragmatic policies in the name of political realism. "You Marxists live in a world of theory," they say. "We live in the 'real' world."

Little do these pragmatic opportunists imagine that they are the most unrealistic of politicians. Their conception of reality is based on superficial appraisals of events, calculations of short-term advantages and a substantial dose of self-deception—not on a scientific insight into the laws of the class struggle and its political dynamics.

All the arguments advanced by the opportunists in support of Kerry contribute, whatever their intention, to the political disorientation of the working class. They leave the working class utterly unprepared for the aftermath of the election, when it will be confronted—regardless of who wins the election—with an immense intensification of political, economic and social crises.

The failure of the working class to free itself from the domination of the Democratic Party during the decades-long death agony of liberalism represents a historical tragedy. The last 35 years have witnessed the unstoppable evolution of the Democratic Party ever further to the right. This evolution arises principally from the weakening of the world position of American capitalism, which has undermined the material basis for the sort of social reformist liberalism that formed the basis of the Democratic Party's appeal to the working class.

Combined with major changes in the social structure of American society, which includes a significant enrichment of those sections of the professional upper middle class (especially lawyers, university academics, etc.) from which the Democratic Party has traditionally recruited its political representatives, the general crisis of American capitalism has all but eliminated the constituency for liberal reformism within the capitalist class and its social periphery.

So advanced is the political decomposition of American liberalism that the Democratic Party is incapable of even mounting a serious political fight against the Bush administration. It cannot and will not articulate the antiwar sentiments of broad sections of working people. Quite the opposite: the principal aim of the Democratic Party has been to block the expression of political opposition to the war. The total disenfranchisement of the antiwar constituency, through the selection of Kerry as the Democratic presidential nominee, demonstrated the degree to which the official political parties are completely independent of the broad masses in the United States. The concentration of political power in the hands of the two bourgeois parties complements the concentration of national wealth in the very small social strata that constitute the American ruling elite.

SOCIAL POLARIZATION AND THE CONCENTRATION OF WEALTH IN THE UNITED STATES

It is impossible to understand the political situation in the United States without examining the most important feature of American society: the extreme concentration of wealth and the corresponding growth of inequality.

In June of this year, the death of Ronald Reagan evoked an extraordinary response within the ruling elite. Much more than maudlin sentimentality was involved in the effusive tributes. Rather, the death of Reagan provided the establishment an occasion to reflect on the changes in American society that have occurred over the last quarter century—that is, since the election of Reagan to the presidency in 1980—and to celebrate the staggering growth in its collective wealth.

To assist in a review of this phenomenon, I have collected a number of charts illustrating the concentration of wealth and the growth of social inequality. Not only do they substantiate the extreme levels of inequality that exist today. These statistics provide an insight into the socio-economic background to critical political developments during the past quarter-century.

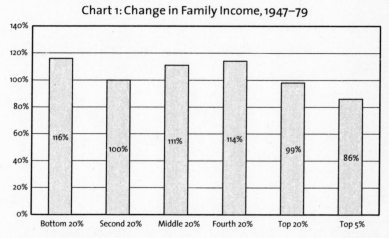

Chart 1: Change in Family Income, 1947–79

SOURCE: Analysis of U.S. Census Bureau data in Economic Policy Institute, *The State of Working America 1994–95*, p. 37.

Chart 1 traces the change in family income between 1947 and 1979. These statistics show that the robust expansion of the American economy in the aftermath of World War II raised the family income of all sections of the population. The families whose income placed them in the lowest 20 percent realized a 116 percent increase in their income. The second 20 percent realized a 100 percent increase. The middle 20 percent saw a 114 percent increase. The top 20 percent experienced a 99 percent increase and the top 5 percent realized an increase in family income of 86 percent. So we see that all sections of the population benefited substantially from the economic growth that followed the war, and, at least in percentage terms, the greatest gains were realized by the lower 80 percent of the people.

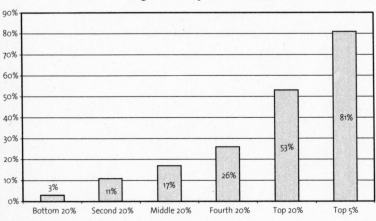

Chart 2: Change in Family Income, 1979–2001

SOURCE: U.S. Census Bureau, Historical Income Tables, Table F–3.

Now let us look at Chart 2, which tracks changes in family income between 1979 and 2001. What an extraordinary difference! We see that the bottom 80 percent of families realized very limited gains, while the wealthiest sections of the population, and especially the top 5 percent, continued to realize a substantial growth in family income. The bottom 20 percent of families realized only a 3 percent gain. The second 20 percent experienced an 11 percent gain. The middle 20 percent realized a 17 percent gain, and the fourth 20 percent enjoyed a 26 percent gain. But the top 20 percent saw its income rise by 53 percent, and, from within that group, the family income of the top 5 percent rose by 81 percent.

Chart 3: Change in After-Tax Family Income, 1979–1997

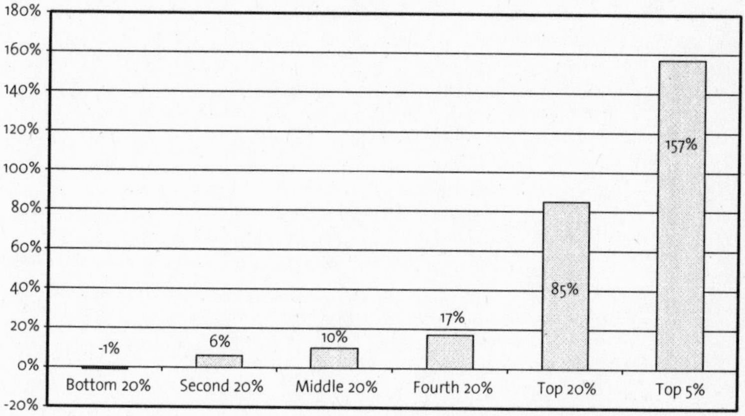

Bottom 20%	-1%
Second 20%	6%
Middle 20%	10%
Fourth 20%	17%
Top 20%	85%
Top 5%	157%

SOURCE: Centre on Budget and Policy and Priorities, Washington, DC, May 2001.

If we look at Chart 3, which tracks changes in family income after taxes, the inequality is even more striking. Between 1979 and 1997, the bottom 20 percent saw a 1 percent decline in its family income. The top 5 percent enjoyed a 157 percent increase!

Now let us look at Chart 4, which shows CEO pay as a multiple of average worker pay between 1960 and 2001. In 1960, CEO pay at an average Fortune 100 company was 41 times that of an average factory worker. In 1970, due to a substantial rise in the stock market, that multiple had risen to 79. The 1970s, a decade of extreme economic crisis, which witnessed a massive decline in share values, saw the multiple fall back to 42. Then what happened? By 1990, CEO pay had risen to 85 times the pay of an average worker. By 1996, it was at 209 times. By 2000, it had risen to 531 times!

Chart 4: CEO Pay as a Multiple of Average Worker Pay, 1960–2001

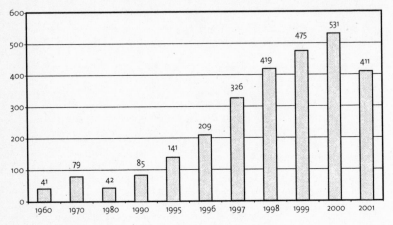

SOURCE: *BusinessWeek*, annual surveys of executive compensation.

Chart 5 shows the distribution of wealth in the United States in the year 2001. The richest 1 percent of the population controls 33 percent of the national wealth. The next 4 percent owns 26 percent. The next 5 percent owns 12 percent. Collectively, the richest 10 percent owns 71 percent of the national wealth. The 10 percent below them owns 13 percent. The next 20 percent owns 11 percent. The middle 20 percent owns just 4 percent. The next 22 percent owns 0.3 percent. The bottom 18 percent has zero or negative net worth.

Chart 6 is especially important. An analysis of the fluctuation in the share of national wealth controlled by the top

Chart 5: Distribution of Wealth in US, 2001

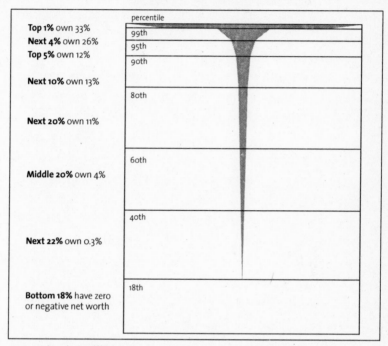

Top 1% own 33%
Next 4% own 26%
Top 5% own 12%

Next 10% own 13%

Next 20% own 11%

Middle 20% own 4%

Next 22% own 0.3%

Bottom 18% have zero
or negative net worth

percentile
99th
95th
90th

80th

60th

40th

18th

SOURCE: Edward N. Wolff, "Changes in Household Wealth in the 1980s and 1990s in the U.S."
Jerome Levy Economics Institute, May, 2004.

Chart 6: Top 1% Share of Household Wealth

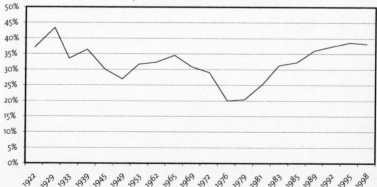

SOURCE: 1922–89: Edward N. Wolff, Top Heavy (New Press: 1996). 1992–98: Edward N. Wolff, "Recent
Trends in Wealth Ownership, 1983–98." Jerome Levy Economics Institute, April 2000.

1 percent of the population provides a profound insight into the social-class dynamics of American history over the last 80 years. After reaching its apogee in 1929, the share of national wealth controlled by the richest 1 percent declined significantly during the 1930s as a result of the depression. It stabilized and rose moderately during the late 1940s, 1950s and at a somewhat greater tempo during the 1960s. It then plunged dramatically in the 1970s—partly due to the gains achieved through the struggles of the working class. But an even greater factor was the impact of the world economic crisis of the 1970s, which resulted in a spectacular collapse in share prices.

This was a consequence of the strange combination of inflation and recession (stagflation), the decline in the profitability of the manufacturing sector and a general loss of confidence within the ruling class. The American bourgeoisie responded to the decline in its social position with a brutal counterattack against the working class.

In 1979, President Jimmy Carter, a Democrat, appointed Paul Volcker as chairman of the Federal Reserve. Volcker dramatically raised interest rates to unprecedented levels, which plunged the US economy into recession.

The conscious aim of this policy was to use mass unemployment to weaken the working class, facilitate a government–corporate assault on trade unionism and lower living standards.

This was spelled out by the leading magazine, *Business-Week*, which wrote in June 1980 that the transformation of American industry "will require sweeping changes in basic institutions, in the framework for economic policy making, and in the way in which the major actors on the economic scene—business, labor, government, and minorities—think about what they put into the economy and what they get out of it. From these changes must come a new social contract between these groups, based on a specific recognition of what each must contribute to accelerating economic growth and what each can expect to receive."[10]

Several months later, Ronald Reagan was elected president and the stage was set for an unprecedented government-sponsored assault on the working class. Its success was guaranteed by the betrayals of the trade union bureaucracy, and its results were reflected in the steadily rising share of national wealth accruing to the richest 1 percent.

A new study by Arthur Kennickell of the Federal Reserve Board shows that the wealthiest 1 percent own about $2.3 trillion in shares of stock, or about 53 percent of all individually or family-held shares. They also own 64 percent of all bonds held by families or individuals.

The reverse image of the spectacular wealth of the elite is the increasingly precarious situation confronting the broad mass of American workers.

An expanding category of the working class is described as the "working poor". According to *BusinessWeek*, "Today, more than 28 million people, about a quarter of the work force between the ages of 18 and 64, earn less than $9.04 an hour, which translates into a full-time salary of $18,800 a year—the income that marks the federal poverty line for a family of four."

BusinessWeek acknowledges that the working poor "labor in a nether-world of maximum insecurity, where one missed bus, one stalled engine, one sick kid means the difference between keeping a job and getting fired, between subsistence and setting off the financial tremors of turned-off telephones and $1,000 emergency room bills that can bury them in a mountain of subprime debt.

"At any moment, a boss pressured to pump profits can slash hours, shortchanging a family's grocery budget—or conversely, force employees to work off the clock, wreaking havoc on child-care plans. Often, as they get close to putting in enough time to qualify for benefits, many see their schedules cut back. The time it takes to don uniforms, go to the bathroom, or take breaks routinely goes unpaid. Complain, and there is always someone younger, cheaper, and newer to the US willing to work for less."[11]

This is the United States of America in the year 2004!

THE AMERICAN CRISIS AND THE WORLD
PROSPECTS FOR SOCIALISM

These extreme levels of wealth concentration and social inequality underlie the breakdown of bourgeois democracy in the United States. The vast expansion of police state measures undertaken by the government during the past three years arises, not from the so-called "terrorist threat", but from the extreme sharpening of social and class tensions within American society.

The most conspicuous and fatal weakness of radical-left, in contrast to Marxist, politics in the United States (and, I might add, internationally) is its inability to conceive of a fundamental crisis of the capitalist system in the United States, or to recognize the working class as the basic revolutionary force in American society. Socially alienated from the working class and politically intoxicated by the media-generated images of American omnipotence, the left-radical milieu sees no objective basis upon which a struggle can be waged against capitalist rule. This accounts for its extreme demoralization, and its feelings of hopeless isolation. It fails completely to see how the interaction of global economic contradictions and intensifying class tensions within the United States is creating conditions for a revolutionary explosion in the very center of world imperialism.

This is not a weakness that is peculiar to the American left. It is an international phenomenon. There are many aspects of this general political crisis on the left. But special emphasis must be placed on its failure to systematically study and assimilate the strategic historical experiences of the struggle for socialism in the twentieth century—in particular, the causes of the degeneration and ultimate collapse of the Soviet Union.

Substantial sections of the petty-bourgeois left view the collapse of the USSR as a demonstration of the failure of socialism and the bankruptcy of a revolutionary perspective based on the working class.

Marxists, however, recognize that the collapse of the USSR and the defeats of the working class during the course of the twentieth century were neither inevitable nor preordained. They were, rather, the consequence of false policies, based on anti-Marxist and reactionary conceptions of a national road to socialism. To Marxists, the present political situation therefore appears very differently, because the lessons drawn from a study of the past furnish the key to understanding the present.

We are approaching an historical anniversary, in which two great advances in theoretical thought will be celebrated. The year 2005 will mark the centenary of Einstein's initial formulation of the theory of relativity, which led to a transformation of man's conception of the universe. It is also the centenary of the 1905 Revolution in Russia—the first great eruption of revolutionary working class struggle in the twentieth century. The events of that year provided the impulse for an immense theoretical advance in the international socialist movement—the formulation of the theory of permanent revolution by Leon Trotsky.

Challenging prevailing nationalistic conceptions that evaluated the prospects for socialism in any given country on the basis of the level of its own industrial development, Trotsky demonstrated that the dynamic impulse for socialism arose from the general development of world economy. The decisive factor in the emergence of a revolutionary crisis in any country was not a particular set of exceptional national conditions, but the contradictions of international capitalism. Moreover, as the causes of socialist revolution lay in global economic conditions, there could be, in the aftermath of the seizure of power by the working class, no national road to socialism. The only viable strategy for the working class was one that conceived of the struggle for, and the building of, socialism as a unified, interdependent, world revolutionary process.

The theoretical and political issues posed by Trotsky's theory of permanent revolution are not merely abstract historical problems. They form the basis for an understanding of the present world situation and the tasks of the working class.

We could, of course, examine at length the manner in which Stalin's conception of a national road to socialism—proclaimed under the banner of "socialism in one country" in opposition to the theory of permanent revolution—led ultimately to the destruction of the USSR. The study of this experience constitutes the basic source of theoretical and political understanding of the fate of the international socialist movement in the twentieth century. Moreover, the catastrophic conditions that prevail in present-day Russia demonstrate the consequences of the betrayal of the international strategy upon which the Bolsheviks based their conquest of power in 1917.

We might also look at the fate of China. It is not so many years ago that radical left tendencies believed that they had discovered, in the banal stupidities of Maoism ("power comes out of the barrel of a gun") the last word in revolutionary thought. Indeed, among Maoist groups all over the world were to be found the most vicious opponents of Trotskyism. And even among radical tendencies that claimed a degree of political sympathy for the ideas of Leon Trotsky, the view was often expressed that the "success" of the Chinese Revolution refuted Trotsky's claims that the building of the Fourth International was essential to the victory of socialism. Had not Mao, and later Ho Chi Minh, not to mention Castro, superseded Trotsky and the old-fashioned concepts, methods, perspectives and strategy of archaic "classical Marxism"? As for the Chinese Trotskyists, who had subjected the bureaucratic character and non-proletarian base of the Maoist party to criticism, and who paid for their theoretical intransigence with decades of imprisonment—were they not hopeless "sectarians", "refugees from the revolution"?

Let us "fast-forward" to the year 2004. What has become of Mao's China? It is the cheap-labor foundation upon which the survival of world capitalism presently depends. Subtract China from the equations of the modern world economy and what would be the present position of American capitalism? In the year 2003, bilateral trade between the United States and China surpassed $190 billion. China is the third largest trading partner of the United States, after Canada and Mexico. The American trade deficit with China totaled $135 billion, the largest deficit it has ever run with any country in history.

American capital is pouring into China, as US capitalists seek to snap up assets that are being sold off by the state and deepen their penetration of the vast internal market.

What is it that attracts American capitalists to China? Their "werewolf" appetite for surplus value and profits are whetted, above all, by the low cost of labor. The Chinese worker earns one-fifteenth to one-twentieth the wage paid to a comparable American or European worker. In the garment industry, which is now dominated by China, the average wage of 40 cents per hour is less than one-third the wage paid to a worker in Mexico. The United Nations estimates that 16.1 percent of Chinese (about 208 million) are paid less than $1.00 a day; and 47.3 percent of the population (about 615 million) live on less than $2.00 per day. This is what makes China, according to the World Bank, one of the most favorable investment climates in the world.[12]

The opening up of China to super exploitation by the imperialists has extracted a terrible social price. While the benefits of imperialist investment accrue to the corrupt milieu of the Chinese state and party bureaucracy, the impact upon hundreds of millions of people—especially in the rural areas—has been nothing short of catastrophic.

When one studies the fate of China and its role in the world economy, it is not an exaggeration to state that Maoism, which is one variant of Stalinism, has made a significant contribution to the survival of American and world capitalism.

However, there is another side to this situation. The very dependence of American and international capital upon China's low-wage labor resources renders it highly vulnerable to the explosive social consequences that must inevitably flow from the super exploitation of that country.

Thus, we are entering into a new period that will be characterized by a growing coincidence of revolutionary class struggle on a world scale. The challenge facing the Marxist movement today is to imbue this world movement with consciousness of its essentially international character, to reanimate it with socialist convictions, and to educate it on the basis of the lessons of the past century. This is the perspective upon which the International Committee of the Fourth International, the *World Socialist Web Site* and the Socialist Equality Party are basing their intervention in the 2004 election.

During the past six months, the Socialist Equality Party has been conducting an intense and vigorous campaign to place its candidates for national, state and local office on the ballot in as many states as possible. It is a difficult process, in which our candidates have been compelled to fight against undemocratic ballot laws designed to prevent third-party candidates from obtaining official ballot status. Many states demand that third parties obtain tens of thousands of signatures, making it all but impossible to appear on the ballot. This year, the Democratic Party is, as a matter of policy, systematically challenging the signatures that appear on the petitions of third-party candidates.

The central purpose of the SEP campaign, however, is not to win votes. Rather, it is to contribute to the political education of the working class, to deepen its understanding of world events and to develop its class consciousness.

Nearly 66 years ago, upon founding the Fourth International, Leon Trotsky said:

"[w]e are not a party as other parties. Our ambition is not only to have more members, more papers, more money in the treasury, more deputies. All that is necessary, but only as a means. Our aim is the full material and spiritual liberation of the toilers and the exploited through the socialist revolution. Nobody will prepare it and nobody will guide it but ourselves."[13]

Two thirds of a century later, that remains the perspective of the International Committee of the Fourth International. But there are no shortcuts to its realization. Socialism is not the sum total of clever tactics, let alone the unconscious by-product of militant trade union demands and protest demonstrations. Such forms of struggle have a role to play, but they are not a substitute for the explicit fight for Marxism. The development of a scientific world revolutionary outlook among a substantial section of class-conscious workers is essential. Socialism can be achieved only through a tireless and unrelenting struggle to explain that there exists no solution to the problems of our epoch other than the conquest of power on a world scale, and, on this basis, the rebuilding of a powerful international socialist culture within the working class.

LECTURE 4

After the 2004 election: the political challenges confronting the American working class

15 November 2004

The political situation within the United States and internationally has been profoundly affected by the results of the 2004 presidential election. The re-election of George W. Bush has come as a shock to broad layers of the population. There is a sense, within the United States and around the world, that something bad, ugly and dangerous has happened.

Prior to Election Day, there was a widespread belief that the outcome of the 2000 Election was a fluke, an aberration that would correct itself, as a sort of natural purgative process, in 2004. All that had occurred during the past four years, in the aftermath of the stolen election of 2000, encouraged the belief that Bush's re-election was inconceivable. The exposure of his various justifications for war as lies, the disastrous consequences of the invasion, the growth of unemployment and accelerating decline in living standards, the widespread sentiment (reflected in the polls) that the United States was headed in the wrong direction: all these and related circumstances were bound to result, so many wanted to believe, in an Election Day repudiation of the Bush administration by the national electorate. This optimistic presentiment was bolstered by the outcome of the three presidential debates, which cast a harsh and unforgiving light on Bush's mental limitations.

These pre-election hopes—which were nourished by large doses of wishful thinking and self-deception—were shattered on November 2, 2004. Back in 1974, following Richard Nixon's resignation at the height of the Watergate scandal, New York columnist Jimmy Breslin wrote a book, *How the Good Guys Finally Won*. The title reflected the complacency of American liberals in the wake of a crisis triggered by the illegal and unconstitutional actions of that Republican president. The malefactor had resigned, and the system had supposedly displayed its resiliency. Three cheers for American Democracy. But this time, 30 years later, the "good guys"—a rather implausible title for the feckless cowards and incompetents of the Democratic Party— didn't win. Rather, an administration, waist-deep in blood and corruption, consisting of political criminals, is back in office. How is this to be explained? This is, of course, not a question for which an easy answer can be found. But to begin with, one must acknowledge that the re-election of George W. Bush has laid bare a deep crisis of American democracy, and American society as a whole, for which there exist neither simple nor conventional solutions.

For the Democratic Party leaders, the cause of their defeat is obvious: their campaign and their candidate wandered too far to the left of the American mainstream. Adapting themselves to the rhetoric of the corporate media, the Democrats find the roots of their disaster in their insufficient sensitivity to the "moral issues" that American voters hold so dear. In a commentary published on November 11 in the *Wall Street Journal*, Dan Gerstein, a former adviser to Senator Joseph Lieberman, writes: "We must realize that many swing voters won't listen to us on the issues—let alone share their votes—if they don't think we share their values."

What are these so-called "values" that the Republican Party has so brilliantly articulated? As the McCarthyite fever of the 1950s subsided and anti-Communism became less potent as an election-winning strategy, the Republican Party sought to develop a new mass base for right-wing economic and social policies by exploiting the political reaction, particularly in the South, against the mass movement of African Americans for their civil rights. The transformation of the South into a bastion of Republicanism dates back to the Goldwater campaign of 1964, when the Republican candidate vehemently opposed the passage of civil rights legislation. Though Goldwater was defeated, his campaign set the stage for the so-called "Southern Strategy" proclaimed in 1968 by the next Republican presidential candidate, Richard Nixon, who recognized the possibility of establishing a new political base in the South by appealing to the backlash against the civil rights movement.

Another critical element of the "values issue", the Democrats insist, is the issue of religion. Here, too, they confess, they must regain the trust of God-fearing Americans. Gerstein writes: "Mr. Bush was able to convince more voters that God was on his side because he was speaking in a vacuum—Mr. Kerry barely talked about religion until the closing days, which helps explain why the Catholic candidate lost the Catholic vote." Even if it were true (and it is not) that the shipwreck of the Democrats was the result of insufficient concern for religious beliefs: it would still be necessary to explain why religion in its most backward, fundamentalist form has come to dominate the politics of the United States. This is a very serious issue, especially when one considers how profoundly the climate has changed since the election of 1960, when the Democratic Party nominated John F. Kennedy as its presidential candidate. He was only the second Catholic to receive the presidential nomination. Thirty-two years earlier, the first Catholic nominee, Governor Alfred E. Smith of New York, had suffered a devastating defeat after a campaign marred by vicious religious bigotry. Given this history, Kennedy was obliged to address forthrightly the issue of religion, which he did in a speech delivered before hundreds of Southern Baptist religious leaders in Houston, Texas, on September 12, 1960.

Kennedy began by expressing regret that it was even necessary to discuss the issue of religion in the America of 1960, when there were so many other critical problems facing the United States, such as "the hungry children I saw in West Virginia, the old people who cannot pay their doctor's bills, the families forced to give up their farms—an America with too many slums, with too few schools, and too late to the moon and outer space." He declared that "These are the real issues which should decide this campaign. And they are not religious issues—for war and hunger and ignorance and despair know no religious barrier." But because his Catholic background had made religion an issue in the campaign, Kennedy accepted that "it is apparently necessary for me to state once again—not what kind of church I believe in for that should be important only to me, but what kind of America I believe in." He then declared: "I believe in an America where the separation of church and state is absolute— where no Catholic prelate would tell the President (should he be a Catholic) how to act and no Protestant minister would tell his parishioners for whom to vote ..."

Kennedy further stated that his conception of America was one in which "no public official either requests or accepts instruction on public policy from the Pope, the National Council of Churches or any other ecclesiastical source" and "where no religious body seeks to impose its will directly or indirectly upon the general populace or the public acts of its officials." He added, "I believe in a President whose views on religion are his own private affair ..."

A fairly conventional declaration of consensus opinion on church-state relations within the political establishment in 1960, Kennedy's remarks appear today to be nothing short of heretical. One cannot think of a single prominent figure in the Democratic Party, not to mention the Republican Party, who would dare to state his opposition to religious meddling in political life so forthrightly. Indeed, when Kerry was asked during one of the debates to respond to instructions issued by Catholic bishops to members of their dioceses, that they not vote for the Democratic candidate because of his Senate votes in defense of the right of women to abortions, Kerry stated that he "respected" their opinion. Why has the political climate changed so dramatically? What is the relation between socio-economic changes in the United States in recent decades and the resurgence of religious backwardness? Is there, perhaps, a connection between the extreme economic uncertainty which afflicts tens of millions of American workers and the constantly growing influence of religion?

Questions such as these are not even raised. No effort is made by the Democratic Party leaders to uncover the rational source, in the current conditions of American society, for the spread of the irrational. As far as they are concerned, the religious revival, notwithstanding its reactionary agenda, is to be accepted as an unalterable fact of American political life. This capitulation to political reaction, for which religion provides a useful guise, finds its consummate expression in the following statement by Mr. Gerstein: "The election also confirmed that culture and character are far more important to connecting with voters than policies and programs."

As a summing up of the philosophy that guides a significant section of the Democratic Party, this is a more or less complete confession of political prostration and bankruptcy. If "culture and character" are more important than "policies and programs", what, then, is the purpose of a political party? Even the most casual reflection on the history of the United States exposes the absurdity of Gerstein's nostrum. The colonies of 1776 were chockablock with "policies and programs" over which the founders of the new American republic labored with an obsessive attention to detail. What was the American Civil War if not a world-historical conflict over "policies and programs" centered on the conflict between abolitionism and slavery? In the mid-1890s, the popular opposition to the growing domination of Wall Street over the national economy found programmatic expression in the demand for a silver-based currency. At the turn of the century, reform factions within the bourgeois parties—which by then were under increasing pressure from new socialist tendencies—advanced a "progressive" program with myriad policy initiatives.

Even within the Republican Party, differences over policy were of a magnitude sufficient to produce a split in 1912, with ex-President Theodore Roosevelt breaking with President Taft and forming the so-called "Bull-Moose" Party. That very interesting election year witnessed a four-way contest between Taft, Roosevelt, the Democratic candidate Woodrow Wilson, and the Socialist Party candidate, Eugene V. Debs. Issues of policy and program dominated political debate. The Democrats, under

pressure from the left, adopted a platform at their national convention denouncing the "high Republican tariff" as "the
principal cause of the unequal distribution of wealth," and
labeling it "a system of taxation which makes the rich richer and
the poor poorer ..." It attacked "private monopoly" as "indefen-
sible and intolerable" and condemned the Taft administration
for "compromising with the Standard Oil Company and the
tobacco trust and its failure to invoke the criminal provisions of
the anti-trust law against the officers of those corporations ..."
The platform also endorsed a national income tax, the popular
election of senators, the establishment of a one-term limit on
the presidency and—in what today would appear to be nothing
less than a revolutionary proposal—"the enactment of a law
prohibiting any corporation from contributing to a campaign
fund and any individual from contributing any amount above a
reasonable maximum."

In the 1930s, the Democratic Party advanced the program
of the New Deal and, finally, in its last attempt to advance an
agenda of social reform, the Great Society of the Johnson presidency. I hope it is understood that I refer to these experiences
not to glorify the history of the Democratic Party, which has
always been a bourgeois party committed, in the final analysis,
to the defense of capitalist interests. The socialist movement in
the United States, from its inception, has devoted no small portion of its intellectual labors to a thorough critique of the
Democratic Party's essentially bourgeois character, the inadequate and limited character of its reformist experiments, and
the falsity of its claim to represent the interests of the working
class. However, the magnitude of the political decomposition
of the Democratic Party can only be understood when placed
in the necessary historical context. Gerstein's contemptuous

dismissal of "policies and programs" is a concise expression of the Democratic Party's complete repudiation of its liberal and reformist past, and its inability to address in any meaningful way the needs and interests of the broad mass of the working class. Indeed, the Democratic Party makes no effort to do so. That is not what it is about.

In his lively and interesting study of contemporary politics, *What's the Matter with Kansas?*, Thomas Frank offers this succinct description of the social orientation and agenda of the Democratic Party:

"The Democratic Leadership Council (DLC), the organization that produced such figures as Bill Clinton, Al Gore, Joe Lieberman, and Terry McAuliffe, has long been pushing the party to forget blue-collar voters and concentrate instead on recruiting affluent, white-collar professionals who are liberal on social issues. The larger interests that the DLC wants desperately to court are corporations, capable of generating campaign contributions far outweighing anything raised by organized labor. The way to collect the votes and—more important—the money of these coveted constituencies, "New Democrats" think, is to stand rock-solid on, say, the pro-choice position while making endless concessions on economic issues, on welfare, NAFTA, Social Security, labor law, privatization, deregulation, and the rest of it. Such Democrats explicitly rule out what they deride as "class warfare" and take great pains to emphasize their friendliness to business interests. Like the conservatives, they take economic issues off the table. As for the working-class voters who were until recently the party's very backbone, the DLC figures they will have nowhere else to go; Democrats will always be marginally better on economic issues than the Republicans. Besides, what politician in this success-worshipping country really wants to be the voice of poor people? Where's the soft money in that?"[1]

To put it somewhat differently, the ideal party supporter, as conceived by the Democrats, is an arbitrageur with a social conscience.

Kerry's problem was not too many programs and policies, but, rather, the absence of any serious proposals to address the great problems confronting the mass of working class Americans. His entire campaign was a protracted and painful exercise in evasion, ambiguity, mixed signals and duplicity. Every concession to the popular base of the Democratic Party was invariably balanced with reassurances to his corporate sponsors. Kerry's belated criticisms of the war in Iraq were accompanied by fervent declarations of his unswerving support for the "war against terror". Yes, he was for increasing the taxes of the very rich ... but not by very much. Yes, he was for the defense of critical social programs, but only if they could be cost-justified on a "pay as you go" basis. Had Kerry's campaign had a motto, it would have been "Absolutely, but not really." The Republicans, with their infallible sense of their opponent's weaknesses and ability to strike at his jugular, knew what they were doing when they mocked Kerry as a "flip-flopper". But Kerry's apparent inability to be clearly for or against anything expressed, not simply his own indecisiveness, but, rather, the basic contradiction of the Democratic Party, that is, of an organization that presents itself as the "party of the people" while faithfully serving the interests of its corporate masters.

There has been a considerable amount of discussion in the recent period of one of the strangest facts of American political life: that many of the states that voted Republican—especially in the South and traditional border regions (Kansas, Missouri,

Kentucky, Tennessee, and West Virginia)—are among the most impoverished in the United States. The impact of Republican economic policies upon the citizens of these states has been devastating. The statistics bear this out: the highest poverty rates, crime rates, divorce rates (despite—or, should we say, because of—the pervasive influence of religion) and other indices of social distress and misery are to be found in the states that voted for Bush. To claim that voters backed the Republicans because of "values" that they hold far dearer than their own real material interests is to substitute mysticism for scientific socio-political analysis.

Abstract references to "values", whose precise meaning is clear to no one, does little to explain why workers have come under the influence of the Republican Party and its retinue of religious hucksters and moralizing conmen. A more convincing explanation is that the virtual collapse of the old labor movement, in states that were once bastions of militant trade unionism, has left millions of workers without any means of confronting social problems and defending their interests as a class. Let us consider the social experience of just one section of the American working class. For much of the twentieth century, the struggles of coalminers, organized inside the United Mine Workers of America (UMWA), raged across West Virginia and Kentucky, as well as significant sections of Virginia, Tennessee, Arkansas, Ohio and even Indiana. The coal miners were arguably the most class conscious section of the American working class. They fought "with fine impartiality"—as John L. Lewis might have said—mighty coal corporations and defied the White House on innumerable occasions. But during the 1980s, the miners suffered a series of devastating defeats, for which the treachery of the union bureaucracy was principally responsible. The UMWA was reduced to a hollow and insignificant shell. Thousands of coal mining jobs were wiped out.

Without jobs, cut off from the deep-rooted social relations that sustained class consciousness over generations of struggle, alienated from a union that had deserted them, the militant workers of yesterday became susceptible to well-practiced pitchmen of the Evangelical Industry, always on the look-out for new customers. For the children of such workers, who have grown up entirely outside the milieu of an organized labor movement and with little or no awareness of the traditions of class struggle, the obstacles to the development of class consciousness are considerable. From what source will they acquire the information and insights that facilitate the development of a critical attitude toward contemporary society, let alone a sense that a better and more humane society—*in this world and in their lifetime*—is possible? Certainly not from the existing political parties or from the cesspool of the mass media.

This does not mean that the average American worker buys into the propaganda to which he or she is subjected relentlessly by the mass media and the Republican political machine. Not by a long shot. They see enough of life to know that things are not as they should be. When a worker speaks of "values", it has a very different meaning for him than it does for Enron's Kenneth Lay or for George W. Bush.

A number of reports has emerged that already call into question the significance of the "values" issue in the 2004 Election. It now appears that the polling data upon which the initial post-election claims were made were either misleading or misinterpreted. This, I am sure, is the case. But the really important point that must be made is that the "values" issue has arisen in a political vacuum created by the absence of any articulation, by either party, of the genuine social, economic and political interests of the broad mass of working Americans. The Democrats, the Republicans and the mass media form different parts of one massive chorus that sings rapturous hymns to the glories of American capitalism.

This is not a temporary weakness that can be overcome through a reshuffling of personnel or the recruitment of better candidates. It is a product of the evolution of American capitalism, the extraordinary concentration of wealth in relatively few hands, the extreme levels of social inequality, the rapid decline of the traditional "middle class" strata that once served as arbitrators in the class struggle between capitalists and workers, and which formed a substantial constituency for social reformism, and, finally, the disappearance within the ruling elite itself of any substantial bloc seriously committed to the maintenance of traditional bourgeois democratic forms of rule.

This very advanced stage of bourgeois democratic decrepitude is inextricably bound up with the metastatic spread of American imperialism, which manifests itself not only in violent predations upon foreign countries, but also in the internal corrosion of all the traditional institutions of bourgeois democracy within the United States itself. In one way or another, the personal wealth and general material interests of every section of the ruling elite, and its substantial upper-class social periphery, depend upon America's domination of the world capitalist economy. This forms the basis for the consensus that exists within broad sections of the ruling elite, supporting the aggressive use of the military to achieve the global strategic objectives of the United States.

Had it been up to the key strategists of the Democratic Party, the issue of Iraq would never have been raised during the election campaign. Following the defeat of Howard Dean's bid for the Democratic nomination, it was the intention of Kerry and his advisors to pretend that Iraq did not exist. There was to be no criticism of the invasion, let alone the so-called "war against terror" as a whole. Even as Kerry's standing in the polls fell dramatically after the Democratic Convention—which was largely a reflection of disillusionment among Democratic supporters over Kerry's refusal to speak out against the invasion—the candidate remained silent.

Not until mid-September, when chaos in Iraq led a number of key Republicans to criticize Bush's handling of the war, did Kerry decide that it was now politically legitimate, from the standpoint of the ruling elite, to make the war an issue in the presidential campaign. And even then, Kerry was careful to distinguish his criticism of Bush's "premature" invasion of Iraq from any suggestion that he favored or, if elected, would sanction, any withdrawal of American troops. Had Kerry been elected, the gory headlines of the past week would not have been any different. He would have endorsed, without any hint of criticism, the onslaught against Fallujah. While making, perhaps, certain tactical accommodations to the European governments to gain broader support for the American occupation of Iraq, the basic course of American international policy would have proceeded under a Kerry administration without any significant change.

Following the election, amidst anxiety and apprehension about the future, there is a widespread sense that a turning point has been reached—that political life cannot continue as it has until now. The symptoms of a historic crisis of American democracy are too numerous and pervasive to be denied and covered over, and it has become all too clear that the system cannot correct itself. The crisis of American capitalism, unless resolved through the intervention of the great mass of the working people of the United States on the basis of a new, genuinely progressive and democratic, that is, *socialist* program, threatens to engulf the entire planet in a catastrophe.

THE AMERICAN WORKING CLASS AND THE DEMOCRATIC PARTY

There are certain political conclusions that must be drawn from the debacle of the 2004 Election. The first of these is that this election must be the last in which the fate of the American working class is tied to the stinking corpse of the corporate-controlled two-party system and, in particular, the Democratic Party. For American workers, political wisdom begins with the understanding that their class interests cannot be achieved through the medium of a party that is controlled by, and subservient to, corporate interests; that their most pressing task is to organize themselves as a politically independent force, in a party of their own, armed with a platform and program that clearly articulates their needs and aspirations.

Viewed historically, the greatest weakness of the American workers' movement has been its subordination to the Democratic Party. This alliance was justified by political opportunists of various stripes—within the bureaucracies of the trade unions, by liberals, and innumerable radical tendencies—who claimed that the Democrats were "friends of labor" whose commitment to social reform would raise the living standards and secure the democratic rights of the working class.

In an earlier historical period, these claims seemed plausible to many workers. For the generation of workers and large

sections of the middle class who had lived through the Crash of
1929, the transition from Herbert Hoover to Franklin Roosevelt
represented a significant change. The "Coming of the New
Deal", to borrow the phrase of liberal historian Arthur
Schlesinger, Jr., marked the beginning of an era of social
reformism that led, over time, to a substantial improvement in
the living conditions of tens of millions of Americans. Measures
that had been rejected prior to 1933 as incompatible with
"laissez-faire" capitalism—such as deficit spending, price sup-
ports for agriculture, official government recognition of the
right of workers to organize and join unions, the introduction of
social security, and the establishment of numerous regulatory
agencies that placed certain legal restraints on the business
practices of corporations—marked a profound change in the
social climate of the United States. But Roosevelt was neither a
revolutionary nor a socialist. He was, rather, an immensely
skilled and farsighted bourgeois political leader who realized
that capitalism would not survive the crisis of the 1930s unless
it was reformed.

Roosevelt's "New Deal" experiments would not have been
possible, however, were it not for the fact that the United States
still possessed immense economic resources. There existed
sufficient financial reserves to sustain a program of class compromise and accommodation. But even then, Roosevelt's desire,
which was no doubt sincere, to create a more just society ran up
against the realities of capitalism. In his State of the Union
address of January 1944, Roosevelt called for the creation of a
second Bill of Rights "under which a new basis of security and
prosperity can be established for all regardless of station, race
or creed." Among the social and economic rights that were to be
guaranteed by the United States to all its citizens were "The

right to a useful and remunerative job," "The right to earn enough to provide adequate food and clothing and recreation," "The right of every family to a decent home," "The right to adequate medical care and opportunity to enjoy and achieve good health," "The right to adequate protection from the economic fears of old age, sickness, accident, and unemployment," and "The right to a good education." Roosevelt asked Congress "to explore the means for implementing this economic bill of rights—for it is definitely the responsibility of the Congress to do so."

Roosevelt's second Bill of Rights was never enacted and none of the proposals that he presented as rights to which all citizens are entitled have ever been realized. The three decades that followed Roosevelt's death in April 1945 witnessed a colossal expansion of American capitalism, which emerged from World War II as the greatest economic power and wealthiest country in the world. And yet, even under those optimal conditions, Roosevelt's vision could not be reconciled with the economic imperatives of American capitalism. Twenty years later, in May 1964, President Lyndon Johnson, the last president to advance an ambitious agenda of social reform, unveiled his proposals for the realization of a "Great Society". But by that time, the global position of US capitalism was already in decline, its trade balance was deteriorating, and its currency was weakening. The added strain of the Vietnam War on the federal budget dramatically undermined the financial basis for the implementation of an ambitious program of social reform. The "Great Society" died in its infancy.

In the 40 years since Johnson proclaimed the advent of the "Great Society", successive presidential administrations, Republican and Democrat alike, have sought to undermine and dismantle whatever has remained of its legacy, as well as that of the New Deal. This process of social and political reaction cannot be adequately explained as the result of the evil intentions of one or another president. Its real cause lies in the objective contradictions of the capitalist system.

The growing political tensions within the United States, the epicenter of world capitalism, are symptoms of the breakdown of a socio-economic system based on private ownership of the means of production, and organized internationally within the framework of inter-dependent, but mutually hostile, nation-states.

An immense development of industry and technology has given rise to a global and mass society, whose complexity requires a level of international coordination and conscious social planning that is inconceivable under capitalism. How is it possible to resolve what are basically world problems when the planet is divided into competing national states? How is it possible to satisfy the needs of billions of human beings—for nourishment, education, housing, health care, and myriad other social necessities—within the framework of an economic system in which considerations of corporate profit and personal wealth determine the allocation of critical financial resources? These problems cannot be solved on the basis of capitalism. The dictatorship of transnational corporations, ruled by financial oligarchs, must be ended. A new, collective, and genuinely democratic means of allocating resources and meeting social needs is required.

The fight for such a program presupposes the building of a new, socialist and internationalist, political party of the working class. This perspective, however, stands in stark contrast to that of the myriad radical tendencies who, to a lesser or greater degree, regardless of this or that criticism of the two-party system, conceived of their political intervention in 2004 as a means of applying pressure to the Democratic Party, of moving it to the left. This was certainly the aim of Nader and the other official candidate of the Green Party. This outlook found its most bankrupt, and even delusional, expression in the political line of the *Nation*, which on the eve of the election published a ringing endorsement of John Kerry. It praised him as "a man of high intelligence, deep knowledge and great resolve." But aside from his personal qualities, Kerry's election, argued the *Nation*, was the only way democracy could be defended in the United States. The re-election of Bush would pose a threat to constitutional rule in the United States. Only by electing Kerry could this danger be averted.

Time does not permit a detailed critique of the *Nation's* position.[2] I will confine myself to pointing out that its line rejects the most important lessons that have arisen out of the tragedies of the twentieth century. As the experience of European fascism demonstrated in the 1930s, efforts by the working class to defend its democratic rights require its independent political mobilization. It cannot fight the threat of dictatorship as long as it remains politically subservient to the parties of the ruling elite. To advise workers that they entrust the defense of their democratic rights to the Democratic Party—which the *Nation* describes, in the same editorial, as "reluctant imperialists"—is to counsel suicide.

It is hardly surprising that the response of the *Nation* to the re-election of Bush is panic and despair. In an article which bears the title, "Mourn", Katha Pollitt hurls verbal thunderbolts at the American people as a whole. John Kerry, she writes, "was a pretty good candidate." The problem is that "the voters chose what they actually want: Nationalism, pre-emptive war, order not justice, 'safety' through torture, backlash against women and gays, a gulf between haves and have-nots, government largesse for their churches and a my-way-or-the-highway president."

While Pollitt denounces the American people for not being worthy of John Kerry's efforts, the editors of the *Nation* lament on another page: "At no time during the campaign did the Democratic candidate discuss in an honest way the single most important issue facing the country: how to disengage from the war in Iraq." Nor, they acknowledge, was Kerry able to address the real social concerns of workers. "He did not offer plausible remedies to their pain." Despite these failures, the *Nation*'s editors reaffirm their commitment to influencing the Democratic Party. "Historically," writes the *Nation*, "that party's finest moments have come when it was pushed into action from outside by popular movements, from the labor movement to the civil rights movement to the women's movement to the gay-rights movement." [3]

The Socialist Equality Party rejects entirely this analysis and perspective. Only by breaking unequivocally and irrevocably with the Democratic Party can the working class move forward. This break implies not only a change in organizational affiliations, but a profound and thoroughgoing transformation in the political perspective and world view of the working class. It involves a shift from a nationalist to an internationalist perspective; from the resigned acceptance of the permanence of capitalism to the realization of the necessity of socialism; from the mere hope that things may someday change for the better to the fervent advocacy of a revolutionary structuring of American society.

Two factors are working in favor of such a transformation. The first is the objective crisis of capitalism itself, which will provide the working class with no respite from shocks and upheavals. The war will not just go away, let alone remain merely a disturbance on the distant horizon. As always, the horrors of war will spread their shadow over an ever-expanding area, demand ever-greater human sacrifices and accelerate the erosion of rights at home. Nor will the accumulating global contradictions of the capitalist system permit a respite from the ongoing attacks on the living standards of the working class. The precipitous decline of the US dollar in the aftermath of the election is a harbinger of worsening economic instability. The chaos generated by the worsening crisis will confront workers with the necessity of defending their most basic social interests.

The second factor is of a subjective character: that is, the efforts of the Socialist Equality Party, the *World Socialist Web Site* and the International Committee of the Fourth International, to educate a new generation of working people and students in the principles of socialism; and to provide a clear political orientation to the working class as a whole as it enters into struggles of an historic character. In the days that have followed the election, we have received scores of letters from readers of the *World Socialist Web Site* in which a wide range of attitudes and emotions find expression ... outrage, disgust, confusion, bitterness and sorrow. Some letters combine all these elements. But most of the letters express a desire to fight back, and recognize the need to re-examine, and probably change, their own political conceptions. The results of the election have shaken things up.

We neither deny nor minimize the difficulties that will arise in the struggle for socialism in the United States. The impact of decades of anti-Communist propaganda and witch hunting, the corruption and betrayals of the trade unions, the relative absence of a politically-engaged intelligentsia, the low level of popular culture and the degrading influence of the mass media, the traditions of national insularity, the persistence of "rugged individualism" and the pragmatic disdain for history and theoretical generalizations—all these are factors which complicate the struggle for socialist class consciousness.

But we take as our point of departure the objective implications of the crisis of American and world capitalism. However complicated the process, social being does, in the final analysis, determine social consciousness. As Leon Trotsky once said so well, history will in the long run cut a path to the consciousness of the working class. American workers will find no other way to solve the problems arising out of the crisis of capitalism except along the path of socialism and internationalism. All other paths lead to catastrophe. That is the alternative that confronts the working class. The responsibility of the Socialist Equality Party and the *World Socialist Web Site* is to confront the working class, as clearly and precisely as we can, with this alternative. As long as we do this, we can leave it to the working class to decide which alternative it prefers.

APPENDICES

APPENDIX ONE
Ronald Reagan
(1911–2004): an obituary

9 June 2004

His Grace! impossible! what, dead?
Of old age too, and in his bed! ...
'Twas time in conscience he should die!
This world he cumber'd long enough;
He burnt his candle to the snuff;
And that's the reason, some folks think,
He left behind so great a stink."

Jonathan Swift,
from "A Satirical Elegy on the Death of a Late Famous General"

It was inevitable that the death of Ronald Reagan, when it finally came, would be greeted with an effusion of saccharine tributes to the 40th President of the United States. But nothing could have quite prepared the innocent bystander for the eruption of dishonest, cynical and preposterously stupid propaganda with which the media and political establishment have responded to the death of Reagan. Of course, given the unending stream of bad news pouring out of Iraq and other parts of the real world during the past year, the Bush administration and its friends in the media were looking desperately for some way to change the subject and counter the increasingly depressed and surly mood in the country. The memorial celebrations of the 60th anniversary of D-Day were intended originally to create that diversion. But the timely death of Reagan has provided an even greater opportunity for an explosion of media-sponsored hero-worshipping, flag-waving and mythmaking.

One is compelled to admit that there is nothing quite so awesome to behold as the total mobilization of the American media. Since the announcement of Reagan's death on Saturday, June 5, the massive weight of this propaganda machine has been set into motion in what amounts to a vast exercise in historical falsification. The modern media version of the air-brush is being applied to the years of the Reagan administration. The social misery in the United States caused by Reagan's policies; the tens of thousands of lives lost in Central America at the hands of fascist death squads funded illegally by his government; the rampant criminality in an administration that was the most corrupt in twentieth century America—all this and other similarly smelly details are being more or less ignored. One reads nothing of his defense of apartheid in South Africa, his funding of countless right-wing dictatorships, or even of his tribute to SS soldiers buried in a cemetery in Bitburg, Germany. The media strives to suppress any objective appraisal of Reagan's life and political career, and to censor reference to the more unsavory elements of his administration's policies.

The aim of this unrelenting propaganda is not only to mislead and confuse, but also to intimidate public opinion, fostering a sense of political and social isolation among countless Americans who despised Reagan and everything he represented and creating in their minds, if not doubt about their *own* judgment, then at least a sense of futility about the prospects for dissenting views in the United States.

But the entire affair—the five days of official mourning, the endless media coverage, the spectacle of a state funeral—leaves the country cold. On Monday morning, in the schools, in offices and factories, there was little indication that the citizenry felt that they had witnessed the passing of a great and significant man, that they, as individuals and as a people, had suffered a genuine loss. For those old enough to remember the death of Roosevelt, let alone that of Kennedy, the contrast could not have been starker. Yes, those men, too, were bourgeois politicians and defenders of the existing social order. But Roosevelt and Kennedy had with genuine eloquence given voice, at different stages of their political careers, to the democratic aspirations of the working class and other oppressed strata of American society; and won for themselves an affection that was deeply felt. Real tears were shed when those men died.

For the great mass of ordinary working people, the death of Ronald Reagan is a non-event. It makes no claim whatever upon their emotions. This is not only because Reagan had been out of the public eye for a decade, since the announcement that he was suffering from Alzheimer's Disease. Too many working people still remember the impact of "Reaganomics" on their lives, which was entirely for the worse. Indeed, among broad sections of the working class he was the most hated president since Herbert Hoover. Even taking into account the support for Reaganism among significant sections of the middle class and more affluent layers of workers, the overwhelming popularity attributed to Reagan was largely of a synthetic character, a myth concocted by the media to endow the policies of his administration with an aura of public approval that they lacked in reality.

As the media repackages history to serve the purposes of the ruling elite, no mention is made of the fact that the 1980s was the decade that witnessed the most bitter episodes of class struggle in the United States since the 1940s. The actions taken by the Reagan administration during its first year in office—the slashing of federal funding for vital social programs and the firing of nearly 12,000 air traffic controllers who went out on strike in August 1981—outraged millions of workers. The social philosophy of the new administration found its most poignant expression in the redefinition of ketchup as a vegetable in order to justify the cutting of federal funds for school lunch programs. In September 1981, nearly three-quarters of a million workers demonstrated in Washington to protest budget cuts and the destruction of PATCO, the union of the air traffic controllers. An even larger demonstration took place in Washington in 1983. Virtually every industry was shaken by bitter and often violent strikes as workers fought back against the class war policies of the Reagan administration.

Apparently that history has no place in the on-going eulogies to the dead president. These tributes to Reagan are, in essence, a celebration of the services he rendered to the rich. The overriding goal of his administration was the removal of all legal restraints on the accumulation of personal wealth. The motto of the Reagan administration, like that of the notoriously corrupt government of King Louis-Philippe in nineteenth century France, was "Enrich yourself". The slashing of tax rates for the wealthy—from 70 percent to 28 percent—earned for the president the boundless affection of the grateful rich. This massive cut in taxes laid the foundations for the environment of social debauchery and orgiastic celebration of wealth that characterized the 1980s. It was the decade of Michael Milken, Ivan

Boesky, Donald Trump (who is now making a comeback), and, of course, the fictional Gordon Gekko, who so famously proclaimed, "Greed is good"!

Reagan is eulogized endlessly as the "Great Communicator". This is the moniker bestowed on him by a media controlled by rich philistines who enjoyed hearing their self-serving platitudes mouthed by the president. The typical Reagan speech was a mixture of hokum, bunkum, flapdoodle and balderdash of the type dished out daily by motivational speakers, along with mashed potatoes and turgid chicken breasts, at countless business luncheons in the Marriotts, Hyatts and Hiltons of America. The same sort of language turned Warren Harding—the 29th President who most resembles Reagan, in both physical appearance and intellectual capacity—into a national laughing stock.

But what sort of man was Reagan himself? Even his most ardent admirers are hard pressed to identify those elements of his personality and character that were in any way unusual, let alone outstanding. His official biographer, Edmond Morris, became so frustrated in his search for the "real" Reagan, the essential man behind the public persona, that he felt compelled to resort to the devices of fiction writing.

The biographer was confounded by the sheer shallowness of his subject. Watch, if you have a chance, Reagan's movies. The pedestrian work of the actor revealed not a trace of creative imagination. The most remarkable feature of his acting was the utter absence of emotional depth. A more sensitive and empathetic man would have found in his own early life—the son of an alcoholic father, reared in the stultifying environment of small town Dixon, Illinois, beneath the shadow of impending financial calamity—sufficient material for dramatic insight into the human predicament. Reagan, however, operated in the realm of the obvious. His acting repertoire consisted of a tool-kit of predictable gestures, which he called upon as required by the dramatic situation. If his character needed to express per-turbation, Reagan furrowed his brow. Anger was conveyed by the stiffening of facial muscles. He was also able to project a cer-tain amount of boyish charm, at least into the early 1940s. But then, as he entered middle age, Reagan's career had begun to stagnate.

During his first decade in Hollywood, Reagan was, if we accept his own description, a "hemophiliac" liberal and sup-porter of Roosevelt. He never offered a credible explanation for the dramatic change in his political views, but it seems to have developed as something of a visceral and angry reaction to the decline of his acting career in the late 1940s. The rightward-shifting winds of the period gave him an opportunity to strike back at high-brow "Reds" among directors and screenwriters who had failed to provide him with the roles to which he felt entitled. This was the real emotional background to Reagan's involvement in the anti-communist Hollywood witchhunts of the late 1940s and early 1950s. Though he publicly denied naming names of suspected members of the Communist Party, it has since been established conclusively that he secretly pro-vided information to the FBI. To Reagan's anger over the failure of his acting career was added resentment over claims made by the Internal Revenue Service on his personal income. These emotions were genuine and deeply felt, and this enabled Reagan to articulate, with a sincerity lacking in all his screen roles, the frustrations and resentments of broader sections of the middle class in the California of the early 1960s.

Notwithstanding his election as governor of California in

1966, his pursuit of the Republican presidential nomination ended in failure twice prior to his success in 1980. But even then, his election to the presidency would have been inconceivable but for the political bankruptcy of American liberalism and the Democratic Party. While the Vietnam War left liberalism and the Democratic Party morally discredited, the worsening economic conditions of the 1970s, eroded the foundations that had sustained the limited social reformism of the Roosevelt administration and his Democratic successors.

During the four years of the Carter administration, the Democratic Party had destroyed whatever was left of its reputation as the party of social progress and reform. While broad layers of the middle class were alienated by inflation, which intensified their resentment of taxes and social welfare programs, the Carter administration adopted an openly hostile attitude toward the working class, exemplified by its invocation of the Taft-Hartley Act in 1978 in an attempt to break the powerful coal miners' strike of 1977–78.

The prostration of the Democratic Party cleared the way for Reagan's election in 1980. But the future successes of this administration would not have been possible without the role played by the AFL-CIO, United Auto Workers, and other trade union organizations in sabotaging the efforts of the working class to resist the assault on their living standards, social interests and democratic rights that followed the inauguration of Reagan in January 1981.

The critical test of the Reagan administration—and, more significantly, the turning point in class relations in the United States—came with the strike of nearly 12,000 members of the Professional Air Traffic Controllers Organization (PATCO) in August 1981. Ironically, PATCO had endorsed the election of

Reagan the previous year, after being told privately that a Republican administration would respond favorably to the union's demands for improved wages and working conditions. However, in accordance with plans that had actually been drawn up during the Carter administration, Reagan announced that he would fire all controllers who did not return to work within 48 hours. There is ample reason to believe that the Reagan administration received assurances from the AFL-CIO that the labor federation would take no action in support of PATCO. There was widespread sentiment among rank-and-file trade unionists for solidarity action to prevent the destruction of PATCO. Had the AFL-CIO ordered industrial action in support of the air traffic controllers, the Reagan administration would have been forced to retreat, thereby suffering a devastating defeat early in its first term.

What transpired was that the demands for solidarity action were rejected by the AFL-CIO; four leaders of PATCO went to jail; nearly 12,000 air traffic controllers lost their jobs; and the union was destroyed.

This set the pattern that was followed again and again throughout the 1980s. Bitter strikes were fought by coal miners, steel workers, bus drivers, airline workers, copper miners, auto workers and meatpacking workers. In each and every case, the striking workers were isolated by the national trade union organizations, denied any meaningful support, and consigned, deliberately, to defeat. In the meantime, employers throughout the country pursued their strike-breaking tactics with full confidence that they enjoyed the support of the Reagan administration.

By the time Reagan left office in 1989, the American trade union movement, thanks to the betrayals of the AFL-CIO, had ceased to exist as a social movement.

If the success of Reagan's domestic program was largely the product of the betrayals of the trade union bureaucracy, what is hailed by the media as the crowning achievement of his international anti-communist program—the precipitous collapse of the USSR—had little to do with the policies of his administration. The dissolution of the Soviet Union in December 1991, three years after Reagan left office, was the tragic culmination of decades of political betrayal by the Stalinist bureaucracies that ruled in the USSR and its client states in Eastern Europe.

As subsequent analyses of CIA intelligence reports have convincingly demonstrated, the Reagan administration had no inkling whatever of the depth of the political crisis in the Soviet Union. The infamous "Evil Empire" speech delivered by Reagan in 1983 was based on a grotesque exaggeration of Soviet strength, not to mention a malicious and ridiculous misrepresentation of its global ambitions.

In its absurd trumpeting of Reagan's visionary leadership of America's victory over the Soviet Union in the Cold War, the media has ignored the really crucial question that arises from an examination of United States foreign policy in the 1980s. And that is, what accounted for the decision by the United States to dramatically and provocatively increase tensions with the USSR? Since the conclusion of the Cuban Missile Crisis in October 1962, the United States had sought to avoid confrontation with the USSR. This policy was expanded by Nixon and Kissinger in the early 1970s with the official adoption of "détente" as the basis of US-Soviet relations.

As historians now know, the decision to reverse course and adopt a more confrontational approach to the USSR began in the waning days of the Carter administration, with the decision in the summer of 1979 to provide funding and military support for anti-Soviet guerrillas in Afghanistan in the hope of provoking a military response by the USSR. The Reagan administration continued and escalated this bellicose policy.

The change in course had far less to do with ideology than with the deepening structural problems of world capitalism, manifested in the recurring economic shocks of the 1970s. The bellicosity of the Reagan administration arose, in the final analysis, as a response to the deteriorating world-economic position of American capitalism.

Regardless of one's political attitude toward the policies of the Reagan administration, it is fairly obvious, on the basis of any objective analysis, that its efforts to resolve this crisis had proved manifestly unsuccessful by the mid-1980s. The increasingly frantic and illegal methods employed by the Reagan administration to suppress popular insurgencies in Central America—all in the name of the global struggle against communism—culminated in the eruption of the Iran-Contra scandal in late 1986. The exposure of criminal operations organized by rogue operatives inside the White House, carried out in defiance of laws passed by Congress, left the Reagan administration shaken and bewildered. Reagan's sole defense against criminal charges was that he did not know what was going on in his own administration. In this instance, the claim of ignorance was entirely believable.

The Democratic Party's response was typically listless. While there was vague talk of impeachment, the Democrats did little more than hold a few half-hearted hearings, in which Oliver North was permitted to taunt and insult them.

But the Reagan administration had all but run out of steam, and its troubles were compounded by the financial consequences of tax cuts and massive increases in military spending. In the face of unprecedented deficits, which had transformed the United States into a debtor nation for the first time since 1914, the Reagan administration was compelled to raise taxes and return to a more accommodating line with the USSR.

The subsequent collapse of the USSR, which Reagan had certainly not foreseen, was only tangentially related to the policies pursued by the "Great Communicator" in the early 1980s. It is true that the dramatic rise in US military spending contributed to the economic problems confronting the USSR. But there is little evidence that Reagan's policies were of any particular significance in determining the ultimate fate of the USSR. Rather, the liquidation of the Soviet state was carried out by the bureaucratic elite after it had concluded that this was the only means by which it could defend its material interests in the face of an increasingly restive and hostile working class.

Having made these points, it is not our intention to suggest that Reagan achieved nothing as president, that he left no legacy.

That is not at all the case. Though Reagan has departed this world, the accomplishments of his administration live on and are observable everywhere: in the staggering growth of social inequality in the United States, in the grotesque concentration of wealth in the hands of a small segment of American society, in the shocking decline of literacy and the general level of culture, in the utter putrefaction of the institutions of American democracy, and, finally, in the murderous eruption of American militarism.

That is the legacy of Reaganism.

APPENDIX TWO
Reflections on the 40th anniversary of the Kennedy assassination

By David North and Bill Van Auken
22 November 2003

In November 1963, 37 years before George W. Bush was installed as president by means of a political conspiracy, the assassination of John F. Kennedy demonstrated how a man could be removed from the presidency by conspiratorial means.

Forty years after Kennedy's assassination in Dallas, the facts of the killing have yet to be established and the official version of events is broadly regarded as a cover-up.

The killing of Kennedy was a political crime that requires a political explanation. It is this fundamental principle that the Warren Commission was set up to deny, and that has been obscured for the past four decades.

While many critical forensic questions remain clouded in mystery, the prevailing crises and divisions within America's ruling elite provide the most compelling evidence that Kennedy was the victim of a state conspiracy, targeted by a faction of the ruling establishment itself in an attempt to shift the course of domestic and foreign policy. This crime had deep roots in the political climate of the time and far-reaching implications.

The assassination's anniversary has been marked by the

media with, on the one hand, sentimental hagiography extolling the legend of "Camelot" and, on the other, exercises in vituperation and character assassination from right-wing commentators seeking to dismiss Kennedy as nothing more than a pill-taking, womanizing political incompetent.

What is called for, however, is a sober evaluation of Kennedy as a figure of his time, with the value of 40 years of hindsight. Marxists begin from a class evaluation of politics, recognizing that Kennedy was a representative of the American financial elite, an opponent of the working class and a conscious enemy of socialism.

We also understand, however, that what happened 40 years ago today had its tragic character, both in the life of an individual and in its impact upon broad masses of working people.

The enduring fascination for Kennedy's very brief administration is not an accident. Both the man and his political career expressed, in a concentrated form, the intense social and political contradictions of the era.

Much has been written about Kennedy's personal history and behavior in recent years. One is left almost with a sense of two lives. His public image was the personification of noblesse oblige, a wholesome and vigorous young president with a beautiful wife and young children. There was something undeniably attractive in his personality, a self-deprecating humor and sense of personal fatalism that was born both of tragedy in his own life and the searing experience of the Second World War.

Hidden from view was a man wracked by disease, dependent upon pain killers and pursing a frenetic sex life with prostitutes supplied by the Mafia.

A similar duality was at work in his political life. He was able to deliver speeches that inspired a sense of idealism—no doubt rooted in the political immaturity and illusions of the time—that marked the beginning, for not a few young Americans, of involvement in social struggles that went far beyond anything that the speechmaker ever imagined or desired.

At the same time, he was engaged in horrifying conspiracies involving brutal counterinsurgency campaigns and assassinations around the globe. His administration worked covertly with extreme anti-communists, assassins and criminal elements to pursue US foreign policy aims, forces that bitterly opposed much of his government's policies. In the end, his reliance on such elements facilitated his own assassination.

It is, nonetheless, worth considering the content of some of Kennedy's speeches, if only to see how far American bourgeois politics has degenerated in the course of four decades. It can be said that Kennedy was the last American president who believed that a public speech should have a genuine social and moral content, and appeal to the public on a high intellectual level.

Announcing the opening of talks on a comprehensive nuclear test ban treaty with the Soviet Union and a US moratorium on atmospheric nuclear tests, Kennedy spoke to an audience at American University on June 10, 1963:

"... let us not be blind to our differences—but let us also direct attention to our common interests and to the means by which those differences can be resolved. And if we cannot end now our differences, at least we can help make the world safe for diversity. For, in the final analysis, our most basic common link is that we all inhabit this small planet. We all breathe the same air. We all cherish our children's future. And we are all mortal."

Just a day later, in a televised address to the nation, Kennedy announced that he had ordered federalized national guard units to enforce the desegregation of the University of Alabama and unveiled plans for civil rights legislation banning racial segregation:

"The Negro baby born in America today, regardless of the section of the nation in which he is born, has about one-half as much chance of completing a high school as a white baby born in the same place on the same day, one-third as much chance of completing college, one-third as much chance of becoming a professional man, twice as much chance of becoming unemployed, about one-seventh as much chance of earning $10,000 a year, a life expectancy which is seven years shorter, and the prospects of earning only half as much ...

"One hundred years of delay have passed since President Lincoln freed the slaves, yet their heirs, their grandsons, are not fully free. They are not yet freed from the bonds of injustice. They are not yet freed from social and economic oppression. And this Nation, for all its hopes and all its boasts, will not be fully free until all its citizens are free."

And, in a speech delivered at Amherst College in Massachusetts on October 26, 1963, less than a month before he was killed, Kennedy addressed social inequality in America and the role of the artist in society:

"Privilege is here, and with privilege goes responsibility ... In March 1962, persons of 18 years or older who had not completed high school made up 46 percent of the total labor force, and such persons comprised 64 percent of those who were unemployed. And in 1958, the lowest fifth of the families in the United States had 4.5 percent of the total personal income, the highest fifth, 44.5 percent. There is inherited wealth in this country and also inherited poverty. And unless the graduates of this college and other colleges like it who are given a running start in life—unless they are willing to put back into our society, those talents, the broad sympathy, the understanding, the compassion—unless they are willing to put those qualities back into the service of the Great Republic, then obviously the presuppositions upon which our democracy are based are bound to be fallible ..."

"The artist, however faithful to his personal vision of reality, becomes the last champion of the individual mind and sensibility against an intrusive society and an officious state. The great artist is thus a solitary figure. He has, as Frost said, a lover's quarrel with the world. In pursuing his perceptions of reality, he must often sail against the currents of his time. This is not a popular role. If Robert Frost was much honored in his lifetime, it was because a good many preferred to ignore his darker truths ...

"If sometimes our great artists have been the most critical of our society, it is because their sensitivity and their concern for justice, which must motivate any true artist, makes him aware that our Nation falls short of its highest potential."

Is it possible to imagine a leading political figure speaking in these terms today? Granted, the words in large part were those of gifted speechwriters and intellectuals assembled by Kennedy's administration. But so, too, are speechwriters crafting the political pig grunts uttered by George W. Bush— "either you're with us or against us"—as well as those of the political Lilliputians who make up the current field of Democratic presidential hopefuls.

The idealism and the appeal to social justice and reform had a very definite foundation. The Kennedy era fundamentally represented the high tide of American liberalism.

It is worth noting that only 30 years had passed from the time of Franklin Delano Roosevelt's inauguration in 1933 and the Kennedy assassination, a considerably shorter period than the one that separates the assassination from today. The weight of the social movement that erupted in the 1930s and forced the implementation of the New Deal reforms was still present. Mass trade unions organized by the AFL-CIO still represented a major force in American political life.

American capitalism also stood at the acme of its economic and political power. It had accumulated colossal social wealth, while at the same time there remained a broad base of support for the continuation and deepening of the social reform policies identified with the New Deal.

MOUNTING CONTRADICTIONS AND CONFLICTS

These very foundations, however, were about to be blown apart by immense tensions and contradictions that could not be contained by Kennedy's policies. There existed a chasm between, on the one hand, the hopes inspired by New Dealism and the idealism of Kennedy's speeches among workers, black Americans and intellectuals, and, on the other, the economic system—capitalism—upon which these policies were based.

The popular aspirations of millions for genuine social reform were not sustainable in a system based upon the private ownership of the means of production. Already, by 1963, the dollar had begun to creak under the strains of deepening economic contradictions. Mounting deficits, expanding foreign investment and growing military spending were undermining the domestic prosperity upon which social reformism rested.

Under these conditions, the policies of the Kennedy

administration were themselves marked by sharp contradictions and intense conflicts between rival factions within
America's ruling elite. It was a government that was compelled
to balance between conflicting social forces.

Thus, after mediating a contract between the steelworkers
and the industry in 1962, Kennedy attacked US Steel for raising
prices by six dollars a ton, conducting a public campaign
against the company and opening up a grand jury investigation
against it until it rescinded the hike. At the time he commented,
"My father always told me all businessmen are sons-of-bitches,
but I never believed it until now." Later, he allowed the company
to raise its prices.

By 1963 the administration confronted a struggle for civil
rights that had moved well beyond the bounds of established
politics to become a mass social movement. This generated
explosive tensions within Kennedy's own party, with
Democratic governors like George Wallace of Alabama and Ross
Barnett of Mississippi threatening to organize a virtual insur-
rection against the federal government. Ultimately this conflict
blew the Democrats apart. Kennedy was the last Democratic
president to be elected with the undisputed support of what his
party once hailed as its "solid South" and the last Northeastern
liberal to capture the White House.

American liberalism, both politically and intellectually, was
founded upon a lie. It had survived the social tumult of
the 1930s and 1940s by striking a Faustian bargain with political
reaction. Anti-communism became the prevailing ideology
of the US establishment, embraced by Democratic and
Republican politicians alike.

Behind Kennedy's idealistic speeches lay the ideology of a
mature imperialist power involved in oppression and atrocities

around the world. While singing hymns to the human spirit, the Kennedy administration had both feet firmly planted in mud and blood.

This was an administration remembered for founding both the Peace Corps and the Green Berets. While both were instruments for advancing US interests abroad, one appealed to young Americans for self-sacrifice to aid the world's poor, while the other recruited them to murder these same poor, should they challenge Washington's policies and US corporate interests.

To no small degree, the emphasis on social progress and idealism contained in Kennedy's public appeal was the response of more perceptive and far-sighted sections of the American ruling class to the threat of revolution and the appeal of socialism and communism to masses of oppressed people around the globe.

But how US imperialism would confront this threat was the subject of an enduring conflict within the ruling elite that would ultimately claim Kennedy's life.

First there was the issue of Cuba. Kennedy began his administration by ordering the execution of the plan hatched by his predecessor, Dwight D. Eisenhower, to invade Cuba with an army of CIA-trained right-wing exiles. When these forces suffered a humiliating defeat at the Bay of Pigs in April 1961, Kennedy refused to bail out the invasion force, enraging both the exiles and their CIA sponsors. This debacle was followed by a covert CIA campaign to assassinate Cuba's Fidel Castro with the aid of the Mafia.

In 1962, however, Kennedy ended the Cuban missile crisis by striking a deal with the Soviet Union to remove its missiles in exchange for Washington's pledge not to invade Cuba and to remove its own missiles from Turkey.

This deal, along with the nuclear test ban treaty negotiated with Moscow the following year, was seen by elements within the military and the CIA—not to mention the latter's allies in the Mafia and among the right-wing Cuban exiles—as a fundamental betrayal.

Among the most right-wing sections of the American ruling class, Kennedy's policies, based on the containment of the Soviet Union and nuclear détente, were anathema. While Kennedy was seeking compromise, they wanted a military confrontation to destroy the USSR. The divisions over this policy in the center of the US state were deep and bitter.

Finally, there was the beginning of the protracted US war in Vietnam. Just three weeks before his own assassination came the military coup that ended in the assassination of Vietnamese strongman Ngo Dinh Diem. Kennedy expressed personal horror at the murder, but if taken at face value this horror was compounded by the fact that he bore direct responsibility, having given the green light for the coup to take place.

By the time of his death, the US president confronted a decision to either escalate the US intervention in Vietnam or cut bait. Either course posed potentially catastrophic implications for his administration.

One cannot attribute the course of American political history over the past 40 years to the impact of the Kennedy assassination. Social conflicts within the US itself and contradictions within world capitalism would have exerted their pressures upon a second-term Kennedy administration just as they did on the ill-fated administration of Lyndon Johnson.

Nonetheless, the assassination of Kennedy was a political act whose aim was to shift the policies of the US government to the right. The conspiracy succeeded in accomplishing its aims.

Moreover, it ushered in a period of politics by assassination that effectively eliminated some of the most dynamic leaders of the liberal wing of the Democratic Party and the mass movement for civil rights—Martin Luther King and Robert Kennedy.

Kennedy's death marked the effective end of the Democratic Party as it had emerged from the New Deal. From 1963 onward, liberalism was dead on its feet. Increasingly, the policies of both major parties were marked by a shift to open reaction.

Present-day political life in America represents the victory of the very forces that were involved in—and celebrated—the 1963 assassination. The political underworld of CIA assassins, gangsters and criminal elements within the ruling elite with which the Kennedy administration worked behind the scenes have now come forward to openly claim the levers of state power.

Endnotes

LECTURE 1

1   *World Socialist Web Site*, www.wsws.org.

2   "The impeachment of President Clinton: Is America drifting towards civil war?" World Socialist Web Site. 21 December 1998.

3   Patrick Martin, "Newspaper studies confirm Democrat Gore won Florida vote," *World Socialist Web Site*, 5 February 2001.

4   *Bush v. Gore*, 531 U. S. 98 (2000) (per curiam) decided 12 December 2000.

5   "Election 2000: The best of all possible worlds," *Counterpunch*, 9 November 2000.

6   *Dred Scott v. Sandford*, 19 How. 393 (1857).

7   Paul Craig Roberts, *Washington Times*, 15 November 2000.

8   Bruce Catton and William Catton. *Two Roads to Sumter*. McGraw-Hill Books Company, Inc., New York, 1971, p. 68.

LECTURE 2

1   David North, "The crisis of American capitalism and the war against Iraq," *World Socialist Web Site*, 21 March 2003.

2   *Iraq: One Year After*, Independent Task Force on Post-Conflict Iraq, p. 13.

3   *Transitional Program for World Socialist Revolution*, Pathfinder Press, New York, 1977, p.190.

4   Alan Brinkley, *The End of Reform: New Deal Liberalism in Recession and War*, Vintage Books, New York, 1996, p. 224.

LECTURE 3

1   Zbigniew Brzezinski, *The Grand Chessboard*, Basic Books, New York, 1997, p. 36.

2   G. John Ikenberry, "America and the Ambivalence of Power," *Current History*, November 2003, pp. 377–82.

3   Peter G. Peterson, "Riding for a Fall," *Foreign Affairs*, September/October 2004, p.119.

4   Martin Wolf, *Financial Times*, August 17, 2004.

5   "Riding for a Fall," ibid., p. 112.

6   ibid, p. 113.

7   Michael T. Klare and Daniel Volman, "African Oil and US Security Policy," *Current History*, May 2004.

8   "Manifesto of the Fourth International," *Writings of Leon Trotsky (1939–40)*, Pathfinder Press, New York, 2001, p. 223.

9   Tariq Ali, *Revolution from Above: Where is the Soviet Union Going?*, Hutchinson Press, London, 1988.

10 *BusinessWeek*, 30 June 1980. p. 56.

11 *BusinessWeek*, 31 May 2004, p. 61.

12 Bates Gill and Sue Ann Tay, "Partners and Competitors: Coming to terms with the new US-China economic relationship," *Center for Strategic and International Studies*, April 2004.

13 Leon Trotsky, "The Founding of the Fourth International", *Writings of Leon Trotsky (1938–39)*, Pathfinder Press, New York, 1974, p. 86.

LECTURE 4

1   Thomas Frank, *What's the Matter with Kansas?*, Metropolitan Books, New York, 2004, p.243.

2   See Lecture 2 above, pp. 47–48, re the *Nation*.

3   *Nation*, 22 November 2004.

Index

MEHRING BOOKS ONLINE BOOKSTORE
www.mehring.com

The Heritage We Defend:
A Contribution to the History of the Fourth International
  By David North

Indispensable reading for all those seeking a serious analysis of the central political problems confronting the working class in the latter half of the twentieth century. Written in the form of a Marxist polemic, The Heritage We Defend reviews the political and theoretical disputes inside the Fourth International, the international Marxist movement founded by Leon Trotsky in 1938. An essential component of The Heritage We Defend is a detailed and objective assessment of the political contribution and evolution of James P. Cannon, Trotsky's most important cothinker in the US.

The book is based on extensive research, with detailed references to original documents and programmatic statements from the archives of the Trotskyist movement.　　　　PRICE: $US21.95, £10.00, $A18.95

The Revolution Betrayed: What Is the Soviet Union and Where Is It Going?
  With an introduction by David North

Written by Stalin's greatest political opponent, Trotsky's brilliant analysis of the contradictory state that emerged from the first socialist revolution provides the theoretical framework for comprehending the processes that culminated in the collapse of the Soviet Union.

PRICE: $US21.95, £10, $A18.95

Globalization and the International Working Class
  A Marxist Assessment

This statement by the International Committee of the Fourth International reviews the historical and political significance of globalization. It critically evaluates the experiences of the working class with the national-based perspectives of trade unionism, the national liberation movements and Stalinism.　　　　PRICE: $US14.95, £8.75, $A14.95

MEHRING BOOKS ONLINE BOOKSTORE
www.mehring.com

Art as the Cognition of Life

A collection of essays by Aleksandr Voronsky

Voronsky was an outstanding figure of post-revolutionary Soviet intellectual life, editor of the most important literary journal of the 1920s in the USSR and a supporter of Trotsky and the Left Opposition in the struggle against Stalinism. As a defender of the "fellow-traveler" writers and an opponent of the Proletarian Culture movement, Voronsky was one of the authentic representatives of classical Marxism in the field of literary criticism in the twentieth century. His work speaks very directly to the current crisis of artistic perspective.

In the late 1920s Voronsky was expelled from the Communist Party, arrested, sent into exile, only to be rearrested and executed in 1937 during Stalin's terror. The Stalinist bureaucracy removed his books from Soviet libraries and virtually erased him from Soviet history. After his "rehabilitation" in 1957, several collections of his writings were published in the USSR in heavily censored form. All cuts have been restored for this edition.

This anthology, the first to appear in English, contains Voronsky's major literary critical essays, including "Art as the Cognition of Life, and the Contemporary World", as well as writings on Tolstoy and Freud, newspaper articles, a satire, two letters addressed to his persecutors, and an appendix of six documents crucial to an understanding of the events of the 1920s.   PRICE: $US29.95, £19.99, $A34.95

BRITAIN	AUSTRALIA	UNITED STATES
PO Box 1306	PO Box 367 Bankstown	PO Box 48377
Sheffield, S9 3UW	Sydney, 1885	Oak Park MI, 48237
Tel: 114 244 0055	Tel: (02) 9790 3221	Tel: 248 967 2924
sales@mehringbooks.co.uk	Fax: (02) 9790 3501	sales@mehring.com
	mehring@ozemail.com.au	

WORLD SOCIALIST WEB SITE
www.wsws.org

PUBLISHED BY
THE INTERNATIONAL COMMITTEE
OF THE FOURTH INTERNATIONAL

The World Socialist Web Site is the Internet center of the International Committee of the Fourth International (ICFI). It provides daily analyses and commentary on major world events, as well as reviews and articles on political, economic and social issues, workers struggles around the globe, culture, the arts, science, history and philosophy from a Marxist standpoint.

The WSWS is an invaluable alternative to the mass media and giant news corporations. It provides a critical forum for those interested in historical truth to access the rich heritage of genuine socialist thought and begin discussing the vital questions facing humanity at the beginning of the twenty-first century.

The WSWS also features the online bookstore, Mehring Books Online, which provides facilities for purchasing books and pamphlets on the history, principles and contemporary analysis of the Trotskyist movement.

www.wsws.org   **www.mehring.com**